SEAN MARIE BEE

Seriously, This Is

Online Dating?

How to Love Yourself Harder and Date Smarter

Seriously, This Is Online Dating?
How to Love Yourself Harder and Date Smarter
By: Sean Marie Bee

Copyright © 2022 Sean Marie Wade

ISBN ebook: 979-8-9851645-0-3
ISBN paperback: 979-8-9851645-1-0

Seriously, This Is Online Dating?
How to Love Yourself Harder and Date Smarter

Nonfiction / Self-Help / Relationships

Disclaimer: This book is not intended to provide more than anecdotal information. Understand that the author is not engaged in rendering legal, medical, mental, spiritual, financial, or other professional advice of any kind. If expert assistance is required, the reader should seek professional services. Printed in the USA for worldwide distribution.

Contact Info:
Sean Marie Bee
PO Box 454
Cypress, TX 77410

info@seanmariebee.com
www.seanmariebee.com
www.instagram.com/seanmariebee

This book is dedicated
to every single woman who is close
to giving up on dating but refuses
to give up on love.

CONTENTS

📶 PART ONE. THE ONLINE DATING JOURNEY

📶 PART TWO. THE HEALING JOURNEY

📶 PART THREE. THE NEW DATING JOURNEY

INTRODUCTION

I don't know you, but I'm willing to bet that your online dating experience has been one frustrating event after another, and you're not quite sure what you're doing wrong. I know how you feel because I've been there: match with a guy, have great conversations, and plan a date, only to get crickets on date night and never hear from him again. Yep! I've been ghosted several times.

I can't tell you why it happens—that remains a mystery—but I'll give you some tips throughout this book to lessen the chances of that happening to you. I've heard ladies refer to online dating as soul-sucking, a circus, a roller-coaster ride, and a dumpster fire. Yikes! Do any of those references fit your dating experience? If your answer is yes, I want you to know that it doesn't have to be that way. What if I told you that you have the power to control your experience? It's true. You do have that power, and I'll show you how to activate it.

Imagine a dating experience where you have clearly defined relationship wants, needs, and deal-breakers, attract high-quality men, and no longer waste your time on guys who are all wrong for you. Instead of your emotions, your self-love and confidence (that are through the roof) guide your dating decisions. You have firm boundaries and rules to help you navigate dating like a pro.

After reading this book, you'll no longer have to imagine—you'll have it all.

Look, I've been where you are, frustrated with having experienced one disappointment after another. I approached dating with low confidence, anxious for love, and needing validation. Eventually, I acknowledged my frustrations were the results of my own negative self-beliefs. Then I took a break from dating and did the best thing I've ever done for myself—I embarked on a healing journey and emerged fulfilled and empowered with improved self-love. Now, my mission is to help women tap into the power of self-love to make smarter relationship choices.

In this book, you'll find actual stories of my online dating experiences. The stories are told for the purpose of teaching and coaching based on real-life examples, and they are not at all intended to diminish the character of any of the men included. Therefore, I've changed information such as names and occupations to protect their identities. Here's what you can expect. This book is sectioned into three parts. In Part One: The Online Dating Journey, we'll discuss common dating frustrations like encountering red flags and how to handle or altogether prevent catfishing, ghosting, and situationships. In Part Two: The Healing Journey, we'll go deep into doing the inner work to identify and address underlying issues and negative self-beliefs that prevent us from making good dating decisions. In Part Three: The New Dating Journey, we'll get detailed in defining boundaries, qualities you're looking for in a partner, your relationship wants and needs, and rules to navigate dating with confidence. At the end of most chapters, there will be a journal prompt or short exercise to complete, so have a notebook or journal ready.

This book won't give you the secrets to finding your dream man tomorrow, but it will give you the secrets to loving and valuing yourself enough to make your online dating experience painless and frustration-free while you look to meet that dream man. Finding love isn't easy, especially when you haven't found yourself yet. But I'll help make it a little easier.

MY STORY

I want to tell you about how I ended up using dating apps. I was married for almost fifteen years. I got married at twenty-one and had no idea of the work it would take to have a healthy marriage. Unfortunately, I didn't have many examples of good marriages in my family, and it wasn't long before my marriage became one of those examples. I hung in there for as long as I could with hopes it would change, but I finally accepted that I had done all that I could to make it work. One day, when my ex-husband came home from work, we argued about money (as we often did), and, in the heat of the argument, I yelled, "I can't do this anymore. I want a divorce!" He wasn't surprised. Given the decline in our marriage over the previous years, we had both known we were on our last leg. We divorced, and suddenly I was a thirty-five-year-old single mom of three pre-teen kids.

The transition from having a partner by my side every day for fifteen years to being single and doing everything on my own took some getting used to. Don't get me wrong, I enjoyed some of the perks of being single right away. Aside from my kids, all my space and time were my own. After work, I went home to a peaceful house with no one to argue with, and things in my bedroom remained where I'd last seen them. On weekends, I curled up in the oversized chair in my bedroom with a velvet throw blanket and a bottle of wine and watched Hallmark Channel movies. If you've seen one Hallmark movie, you've seen them all. The guy and girl meet. They pretend not to like each other, and then they fall in love. I knew the ending to each movie before it started, but the love stories that led to the end were the parts I looked forward to. I wanted that fairy-tale love.

But after four months of living single, the honeymoon phase ended. Staying in the house every weekend watching movies got old. A few times, as I watched the Hallmark movies I loved, I caught myself yelling at the television, "No one falls in love in two weeks! That's not reality!" It was time for me to get out of the house and meet people.

One evening, as I was curled up in my comfy chair watching a movie, my friend Rhonda called. She and I hadn't lived in the same city for over five years, but we never lost touch. She asked what I had planned for the weekend, and I told her I would be doing the same thing I had done every weekend for the past four months: curling up in my chair with a bottle of wine and watching movies. Rhonda yelled, "You need a date!" I told her I was fine, though truthfully, single life was getting lonely. But the thought of going out on a date gave me anxiety. My last date had been more than sixteen years ago.

Rhonda told me I needed to try online dating. Now, wait! You may be thinking, *Ugh! I've heard this story before. Your friend made you do it.* But she did—my friend introduced me to online dating, and my response to her was, "No way!" Though I had never tried it, I told her it wasn't for me because I was going to meet someone the natural way, at the gym, the grocery store, or happy hour with my coworkers. Rhonda laughed hysterically and said, "Girl, dating has changed a whole lot since the last time you were on the dating scene. Men rarely approach women these days. They stare at us, smile, and walk away. Then they go online and find women to talk to. Trust me, I know what I'm talking about." I did trust her, but I told her I would take my chances on meeting someone the traditional way. After my talk with Rhonda, I started to notice the pattern she mentioned while I was out in public. Men would look at me, smile, and keep walking. It happened almost every time I went out. I didn't understand it. I'm approachable, and I smiled back. But seemingly that was not enough—until one day when I went to at a restaurant for happy hour and sat across the bar from Craig and his coworkers.

Craig stood at 6'4", muscular and quite handsome. I could hear (and see) his animated personality from across the bar as he dramatically told his coworkers a funny story about a work meeting gone wrong. Craig looked at me a few times and smiled, and I smiled back. Oddly, the bartender asked me if I could move to the vacant seat next to Craig so he could seat a couple together. I obliged and took my new seat. As soon as I sat down, Craig introduced himself. "Hello, miss. My name is Craig. And you are?"

"I'm Sean. Nice to meet you."For an hour, I talked and laughed with Craig and his coworkers until I decided to head out. I said goodbye to the crew, then Craig walked with me outside and said, "I enjoyed your unexpected company. Can I have your phone number so I can call you sometime?"

"Sure."

I knew it! I couldn't wait to tell Rhonda I had met a man at happy hour. I was excited to be possibly going on a date soon. But that excitement was short-lived. On my first phone call with Craig, he invited me to his house for sex. Craig explained that he was not looking for anything serious, and he only had time for friends with benefits. I told him I appreciated his honesty, but I was not interested. That was that. We were over before we started.

After my conversation with Craig, I concluded that online dating couldn't be much worse than getting propositioned for sex after a night at a bar, so I'd give it a try. I figured that, in three to six months, the right man would come along to sweep me off my feet—but I couldn't have been more wrong.

Years later, I was still single and had racked up profiles on thirteen different dating apps. I had been ditched, catfished, ghosted, tricked, stalked, and, if that wasn't enough, I had spent two and a half years stuck in a friends-with-benefits situationship, hoping for a relationship.

Throughout this book, you'll hear the good and bad of how I went about dating, including the behavior I tolerated from men out of loneliness and desperation. Five years into my dating journey, God intervened and guided me off the dating scene and onto a path of healing. As a result, I love myself more, fully know my worth, and live a life free of relying on others for love and validation. The healing process was hard, but it was worth it to come out on the other side as the woman I am today. I haven't found the love of my life yet, but my healing journey has made dating much easier and my single life overall fulfilling. These days, I focus much of my attention on being a self-love and online dating coach to help ladies avoid going through the wild experiences I'm going to share with you. I know that if you take these lessons I share in this book to heart and apply them to your life, you will end up on your own healing journey, and you may even end up in a relationship with the man of your dreams. So, grab your tea, wine, or whatever your comfort drink is, and get ready to laugh, cry, empathize, yell at me, and maybe even learn something as I share my dating and healing journeys with you.

PART ONE

THE ONLINE DATING JOURNEY

Dating Mistakes and Lessons Learned

CHAPTER 1

RED FLAGS: IDENTIFY, ACKNOWLEDGE, AND ADDRESS

How many times in your dating journey has a man said or done something that caused you to pause and ask yourself, *Is this something I should be concerned about*? When you ask this question and have to think twice or even three times about it, it's a sign that what they're saying or doing may be a red flag for you.

Red flags are indicators that you're not comfortable with a person's actions, words, or even their perspective on certain topics. Proceeding with a relationship with a person who is giving off red flag vibes may not be in your best interest. Typically, when we think of red flags, we think of extreme behaviors that would stand out to anyone, but that's not always the case. Obvious red flags like disrespect and anger are easy to spot when displayed, but the subtle ones like love bombing (when a guy shows excessive affection towards you intending to manipulate you into a relationship) or having lingering feelings for an ex may not be so easy to spot at first. The important thing is that when you spot a red flag, you should immediately acknowledge it, address it, and move forward.

Avoid ignoring or making excuses for red flag behaviors. A common excuse that gets inadvertently used for concerning behaviors is that the person had a bad day. If your date slams their fist on a restaurant table or speaks disrespectfully to you because they had a bad day, it may be a sign he has anger issues and violent tendencies. Imagine what would happen if he had a bad *week*. See the behavior for what it is and move on to another guy.

When I started my online dating journey, I wasn't necessarily looking for red flags, but somehow, I hit the jackpot. You'll see, some were obvious and others subtle, but they all were determining factors for me to move on from these guys.

ANGRY VIBES

Thirty-six-year-old Sean Marie had not yet gotten past her desire for a bad boy. I'm not talking about the breaking-the-law type of bad, but the strong, masculine, take-charge type of bad. So, when I saw Angry Man's dating profile, I was intrigued. According to his bio, he was an established entrepreneur ready to settle down. He was six foot two with big arms and a smooth chocolate complexion. *Oooh!* He didn't smile in any of his pictures, but he had this sexy, masculine look in all of them. I couldn't click the like button quick enough on the image of him sitting on a motorcycle with no shirt on, mean-mugging whoever was holding the camera.

Later in the evening, he sent me a message: "Hey, pretty lady."

I subsequently replied, "Hi there." Simple enough.

That's when our two-day dating app chat began. During our chat, Angry Man told me he had a five-month-old baby. That should've been enough information for me to thank him for his time and send him on his way. With a kid that young, it was likely he had just walked away from a serious relationship.

He called me for the first time while he was driving home in rush hour traffic, which would be a bad idea for anyone. I'm mild-mannered, but driving in rush hour traffic in my city makes even me yell out comments I have to repent for later. I told him I was okay with him calling when he made it home, but he insisted on staying on the phone. We were having a pleasant, quiet conversation until, out of nowhere, he yelled, "You stupid son of a . . . ! You don't know me! I will break your legs!" Then, he calmly asked, "How was your day?"

"Uhm, it was good."

I was confused about what I had just *ear-witnessed* and how he was able to go from deranged to calm in three seconds. That was some psychopath stuff.

As I began to tell him about my day, he did it again. He growled explicit words as if he was demon-possessed. I swear, I heard two voices coming out of his mouth. His head was probably spinning like the girl's in *The Exorcist.* I've witnessed road rage before, but that was some next-level stuff.

"Are you okay?" I asked.

"I'm fine, but I hate it when people cut me off. It drives me crazy."

Obviously, I thought. Working in employee relations for many years, I was used to thinking on my feet and handling angry people gently under challenging situations. I sympathized with Angry Man and said, "Wow! I understand how you feel. Well, someone just walked into my office, and I should go help them. I'll have to call you back later."

Angry Man gently replied, "It's all right, sweetheart. Handle your business." I had no intention of calling him ever again.

An hour later, he initiated a text conversation.

Angry Man: wyd *(What you doing?)*
Me: Still working
Angry Man: Question. Are you still sleeping with your ex?
Me: Uhm, no. Why do you ask?

Angry Man: Just making sure you'll be all mine.
Me: You have a five-month-old baby. Are you still sleeping with your ex?

Naturally, a woman would still be attached to her child's father soon after giving birth.

Angry Man: Umm . . . hell no! I hate her f**king guts.
Me: Wow! That's harsh. Do you see the baby?
Angry Man: Naw . . . but hey, I know who my daddy is, so she ain't hurting me at all. More money for my other kids.

I was speechless. Only a vile, disgusting, immature man-boy would make those comments about his infant child and the child's mother. There was no way I was going anywhere near that man or speaking with him ever again. I did what any sensible woman would do: I blocked him. A person like that didn't deserve an explanation of why I didn't want to date him. If I told him the truth, that he was a bum, I'm sure he would've come through the phone and choked me out.

I imagined red flags waving vigorously above Angry Man's hot head. I know tough, masculine men are sexy and make you feel safe, but a man with uncontrollable anger is a ticking time bomb who will ultimately go off on you, as he does on everyone else. Angry Man didn't hold anything back, and I'm glad he didn't. A man like that who speaks disrespectfully about his child's mother (or any woman) won't spare you. It won't be long before he becomes disrespectful toward you. And I don't think you need me to tell you this, but I will. If you ever encounter a man who speaks proudly about abandoning his child, run! He needs serious help.

There was one good thing that came out of my conversation

with Angry Man. In one day, he completely obliterated my desire for a bad boy. I was cured!

EMOTIONALLY UNSTABLE VIBES

Psycho Emoji Man was a recovering workaholic and was ready to settle down and prioritize marriage, but he was much too eager. He talked about love and marriage a little too much. We spoke on the phone for about two weeks before meeting in person. Since I was heading out of town to visit family that same day, our meeting was only twenty minutes. Later that night, things got weird. He sent a text message saying, "I miss your beautiful face already," followed by seven sad face emojis.

For the next two days, Psycho Emoji Man texted me throughout each day, telling me how beautiful I was and how much he missed me. First, it was cute; then, it became excessive. He started calling every couple of hours. I told him to stop because I was trying to enjoy time with my family. When I finally answered his call, he asked me if he could speak with my dad to get his permission to propose.

"Propose what?" I asked.

"Marriage," he said.

"Are you serious?"

"Very serious," he assured me.

"We barely know each other. You're joking, right?"

Psycho Emoji Man said it wasn't a joke, and I was going to be his wife. For ten minutes, we went back and forth in conversation as I explained to him that we did not know each other well enough to be considering a relationship, let alone an engagement. This was not resonating with him, so I told him it was time for us to go our separate ways, and I hung up the phone.

Minutes later, he sent crazy text messages—one after another:

1. We don't have to get married now.
2. Can you hear me out?
3. Why aren't you responding to me?

The messages stopped for a couple of hours, but I could feel that the crazy was brewing. When he resumed messaging, he put some psycho on it. He sent about twenty crying emojis at a time. When I didn't respond to those, he sent twenty-something angry face emojis mixed with hearts and blowing kisses. This continued for days. I wanted to block him, but I didn't because I wanted to get the message if he texted, "I'm standing outside at your door." He didn't know where I lived, but people that crazy are capable of anything.

The psycho text messages went on for a total of nine days. After that, I never heard from Psycho Emoji Man again. That had me looking over my shoulder when I left my house for months.

The red flags here are obvious, but I'll still point them out for you. When someone gives you excessive attention and proclaims their love for you in the first couple of weeks of meeting, something is wrong. They are love bombing you, which is a form of manipulation and control. It's tempting to believe that you finally found a man who fully recognizes how amazing you are, but when he smothers you with affection and shows himself to be unstable at the slightest sign of rejection, run.

BAGGAGE VIBES

You can always spot a wounded man by how he talks about his ex. He will tell you that everything that went wrong in their relationship was her fault, and that he was a victim of circum-stance. He'll never tell you about his part in the relationship's failure because he believes he didn't do anything wrong. It's a complete turnoff.

In my first conversation with Bag Man, he insisted we talk about our exes. I told him the point of our phone call was to get to know more about each other. I wasn't interested in discussing exes and past relationships. We moved on and talked about life and family, but he found a way to fit his ex into the conversation. He said his ex was evil, and she was the reason why he wasn't more advanced in his career. I knew this would not be good, but I wanted to hear the story.

"How did she keep you from advancing your career?" I asked. He said he had found out his ex-wife cheated on him two days before he was offered a big job promotion. He didn't take the new job because it required him to travel for weeks at a time, and he couldn't be away from home that long since he needed to be there to watch his wife.

I considered that maybe what he said had gone over my head, and I needed clarification. So, I said, "She had already cheated on you while you were home. How was not taking the job going to prevent it from happening again?" He ignored my question and continued telling me how horrible a wife his ex was.

"I'm sorry you went through that, but on the brighter side, now you have the opportunity for a new start." (I did try to be a ray of sunshine.)

"Oh, no need to be sorry," he said. "We divorced ten years ago."

"Wow! Have you advanced in your career in the last ten years?"

"Yes, but not as quickly as I could have," he added.

Bag Man went on to bash his ex-wife even more—*poor lady.* I thanked him for the conversation and told him we were not a good match.

"Well, that's not fair," he said. "You didn't even give me a chance."

"I heard enough to know that we won't work out."

In ten years, this man could've had two careers. Instead of

taking responsibility for his lack of professional achievement, he found it convenient to blame his ex-wife. It was apparent he was still holding onto spoiled, ten-year-old baggage. It was beyond stale. A man like this lacks personal accountability and will find fault with everyone but himself. Stay far away from a man who displays this behavior in the slightest. He is miserable, and misery loves company.

GRIEF VIBES

Sorry had no business being on a dating app. He was a sweetheart, but his heart was still with his ex-wife. On our first date, he killed the entire vibe. Sorry lamented over his ex-wife throughout our entire evening. It was painful to listen to. Two years earlier, his ex-wife had left him for her coworker. He didn't want the divorce, but he didn't fight it either. Six months after their divorce was final, the man his ex-wife had left him for kicked her out of his house, and Sorry took her back in until she could find a place to stay.

A year later, she was still living with him. I told him it seemed like he still loved her, and he needed to see if they could work it out. He said, "Oh no, I think you misinterpreted what I've been saying. I don't love her. I'm completely over her." *I* was completely over *him* and that date altogether. The poor guy was delusional. After being divorced for almost two years, he was still in the first stage of grief: denial. As he talked about his ex, he sounded like he was running out of air, and his posture slumped over. I felt sorry for him. At the end of the date, I gave him a big hug and wished him the best.

A man who can't stop speaking about his ex is either not over her or not over the pain of the breakup. Either way, he still has an emotional attachment to her, making him emotionally unavailable to you. He'll never be able to connect with you to form a meaningful relationship until he has allowed himself the time to resolve the issues of the breakup.

JERK VIBES

First impressions are everything when it comes to dating. No matter how amazing you are, if you don't show it the first time, it's likely you'll never get another chance. Opportunities for do-overs are rare.

Bayou Classic didn't get another chance because he was oblivious on the first phone call. We had a good conversation until I told him I was from New Orleans. Lord have mercy. In a ridiculous, fake Cajun accent, Bayou Classic said, "Oh, you're from New Orleans, baby. I love New Orleans, baby. You eat crawfish, baby?"

"What are you doing?" I asked.

Bayou Classic replied, "This is my Baton Rouge accent, baby."

"People in Baton Rouge don't talk with that accent. Please stop!"

He said, "Yes, they do, baby."

Lord have mercy! At first it was funny, but it became annoying. He was mocking my people, and I didn't appreciate it. He finally stopped speaking in that ridiculous accent and talked like he had some sense. By then, it was too late. He had already left a bad taste in my mouth, so I ended the call. I texted him the next day to tell him we were not a good match.

Bayou Classic had zero ability to read the room—or my tone, for that matter. He was oblivious to the fact that he was annoying the hell out of me. I was not laughing at all. I had to beg him three times to stop talking in that stupid accent before he finally ceased the foolishness.

Don't get me wrong, I adore a man who can make me laugh, but a man who pushes the line of joking to being outright offensive is a jerk. His lack of self-awareness pushed him past the point of no return.

SUGAR DADDY VIBES

Gucci was an older man whose dating app profile consisted of two pictures of him and thirteen of his luxurious lifestyle. There were pictures of him driving luxury cars, showing off his diamond bezel jewelry, and vacationing on the beach. The only thing he was missing was a photo with fanned-out money on a mattress. I didn't typically match with men who showed off glamorous lives on dating sites, but that time I figured, *Why not?*

My conversation with Gucci wasn't much different from what I expected. He talked about his material things and embodied high confidence that could easily be mistaken for arrogance, but overall, it was an okay conversation.

Now, men know that most women have a passion for expensive handbags. Too bad for Gucci, I wasn't one of those women. Just when he seemed to be an okay guy, he sent me a picture of himself at the barbershop with a $6,000 Gucci bag, captioned, "If you were mine. Call home!" After an hour passed and I didn't call home, he sent another message. "Must be the wrong color." I told Gucci he had the wrong woman, and he should not bother to call me again.

Ladies, you may think I'm crazy for this one. I know women who would've taken the bag and then some, but Gucci's message was a total turnoff for me. I've never been into men who try to purchase me. Based on my experience with this type of man, he's either controlling or highly insecure. Besides, we all know men are not handing out $6,000 handbags at no cost. There's always a price. Think hard about what you're willing to pay.

FREAKY VIBES

It wasn't often that I came across the profile of a fine, handsome stallion of a man dressed in a nice suit. Dom's pictures showed him in a tailored blue suit that fit his body like a glove. He sent a message to my inbox while I was on my app of choice browsing profiles, and I replied immediately. We chatted on the dating app for a couple of days, until he asked if we could move our conversation over to a messaging app. I wondered why he wanted to switch from one app to another, but he just gave me his username and told me I'd understand why when I saw his profile. That should've been my first red flag.

On the messaging app, Dom's profile picture displayed him in a mirror holding a flogger and wearing a leather mask and leather underwear. I messaged him, "Dom?" His reply was, "Are you surprised?" "Let's just say this is not what I expected," I told him.

I didn't want anything to do with whatever kinky stuff this man was into. Then, Dom asked if I was a sub.

"What's a sub? I may be a snack, but I'm not a sandwich!" "A submissive to a dominant's control," he explained. "You do what I tell you to do, mostly during sex but also in life."

"No, I haven't been a sub, and I'm not interested in becoming one," I replied.

He said he understood that it was not for everybody. I asked why he didn't use a dating site specifically for those relationships. He said he was looking for a clean and wholesome woman to introduce to his world, and I fit the look. Obviously, this man was trying to live out *Fifty Shades of Grey,* but I was not going to be his Anastasia Steele. I didn't judge him. I wished him well in his search and continued with mine.

ABUSIVE VIBES

I had a weird feeling about Looney the first time he messaged me. When I viewed his profile back then, I listened to discernment when it nudged me to keep it moving. A year later though, when he messaged me again, there was no nudge, so I took that as a green light to give him a chance. In our first phone conversation, we found that we were fans of the same football team, which had a game airing a few hours later. Looney suggested we watch the game together on FaceTime as a first date. It was different, but I was cool with it. He planned to call me ten minutes before the kickoff.

When he called, I was in the middle of setting up my new Bluetooth earpiece. I answered his call, and my earpiece disconnected the call when he began talking. Immediately, I called him back and explained what had happened. We started a conversation, and the call was disconnected again. I felt terrible, but I thought, *Surely, he will understand it was a mistake.* When I called back, I expected a little frustration, but I wasn't ready for what was about to happen.

Looney answered the phone in a chastising tone. "What is your problem? Do you know how to work a phone?"

I responded, "Hey, I apologize. I understand that was frustrating, but relax."

In an eerily low, chilling tone, he uttered, "Okay. Don't let it happen again."

Whoa! It felt like he would have backhand slapped me if I had been standing next to him. I told him it was best that we end that call and never speak again. He said, "Yeah, I think that's best." *Looney!*

When something doesn't feel right, nine times out of ten, it's not right. Watch out for the overly critical man who talks down to you and gives you eerie abuser vibes on a phone call.

My struggle with that little earpiece allowed me to see the real Looney, who couldn't control his anger. If he was that upset on a second phone call, I can't imagine what he would have been like if we had been face-to-face on a date.

CONTROLLING VIBES

Mr. Red and I matched on a dating app and immediately hit it off. We chatted on the app throughout the day and scheduled some time to have a phone call the next day after he got home from church. Mr. Red called at our scheduled time. The one positive thing I can say about him is that that man was rawly and unapologetically himself. Ten minutes into the conversation, Mr. Red had used every curse word I could think of. I had zero interest in him by that time, but I was entertained and curious to hear what he would say next.

Mr. Red asked how long I had been married. When I told him fifteen years, he seriously said, "If you were my woman for fifteen years, I would own you. Leaving would not be an option." And that was just the beginning. Mr. Red also asked about my favorite color nail polish. I told him red. He said, "No woman of mine is wearing red nail polish. That is nasty. Red polish looks like your fingers and toes are bleeding."

"Well, good thing I'm not your woman."

"If you were my woman, I would make you get the nail polish remover and wipe it off."

"Wow! That is very controlling."

"I don't care. If you come around me with red nail polish, it is gonna be a problem."

My dad called right on time. I was done with Mr. Red. "My dad is calling, so I have to go," I said.

"Call me when you're done talking."

I had every intention of calling Mr. Red back and letting him know we were not a match, but he got even crazier. He texted, "Hey buddy, what you doing?" I was not available to respond. Thirty minutes later, he sent a bunch of laughing emojis. I had no idea what was going on with him. His filthy mouth and controlling ways were enough, and then he came with this. Red flags were flying in every direction. To avoid any further communication, I did not respond. He never contacted me again, thank God.

You may like your man a little raunchy, and that's okay. What's not okay is a man who believes that he owns you once you're in a relationship and can go as far as dictating what color nail polish you wear. These are serious signs of controlling and abusive behavior.

If you're a pro at spotting red flags and immediately acknowledging and addressing them, that's great. But if you're someone who needs some help in this area, grab your journal and try this exercise. Think over your last three years of dating. What red flag behaviors have you noticed? What did you do when you noticed them? Did you immediately acknowledge them? Did you ignore or make excuses for them? Answer these questions honestly. It's okay if you didn't handle red flag behaviors perfectly in the past. Doing this exercise now will raise your awareness, and, naturally, you'll handle them better in the future.

CHAPTER 2

COLLECT THE DATA AND
DISCOVER THE REAL HIM

Have you ever fallen for a man's representative? In the online dating world, it's easy to get caught up in becoming a little too interested in a guy through conversation, especially if the guy can talk a good game. Men who intend to deceive you will encourage you to do all the talking while they listen . . . and plot. Be leery of the guy who asks lots of questions about you but only utters a few lines when you ask about him. Ladies, I know we get excited when we meet a guy who is interested in learning all about us right away, but a conversation goes two ways. He shouldn't be reluctant to talk about himself if he wants you to spill all the tea about you. If you listen closely, you'll notice that when he opens up about himself after you've told your life story, you will suddenly have a lot in common, and it won't be a coincidence.

Hot Boost flattered me with compliments and attention when we met online. He asked about my passions, hobbies, family, and blood type. Okay, maybe not my blood type, but you see where I'm going with this. Hot Boost checked most of the boxes on my list of must-haves—or so I thought. He boasted about a lucrative real estate investment portfolio and told me all about the renovations in the homes he had recently purchased. We had daily phone calls for two weeks where he talked about his plans to visit wineries in Napa Valley, the limited edition bottles of wine he was bringing back home with him, and the many books on his to-read list. He seemed like my ideal guy.

When I proposed that we plan a face-to-face meeting, Hot Boost claimed he would be out of state checking on the progress of renovations on his rental properties. I proposed another time, and he claimed he would be away on vacation. Since he was always busy, I asked that we have a video call. This is where things took an interesting turn. He said he couldn't do a video call because he couldn't download apps to his phone. Instead, he texted me a blurry picture. When I asked for another one, he said, "That's the best I can do on this hot boost."

I was confused. "What is a hot boost?" He explained that he owned a Boost Mobile prepaid phone. This meant that either he had another phone or he was not a fancy real estate investor. I was not as attentive as I am today, so I didn't immediately recognize the discrepancy.

Hot Boost and I finally found a mutual meeting time and day to meet at a lounge downtown. I arrived at the lounge thirty minutes early and sat at a table outside on the patio. Two gorgeous, well-dressed gentlemen were sitting at the table across from me. As I was eavesdropping on their conversation, I heard one gentleman encouraging the other to come over and introduce himself to me. The one in the tan blazer told his friend, "Say something to her."

After a few minutes of motivation from Tan Blazer, the friend finally came to my table. The sweet scent of his cologne made it to my table before he did. In a smooth, deep tone, he said, "Hello, sweetheart. My name is Jay, and I'd really like the opportunity to get to know you. Are you waiting for someone?"

Realizing I was turning down a handsome, great-smelling

guy, I reluctantly said, "Yes, I'm waiting for a friend." Jay retreated to his table and glanced back at me as he jokingly hung his head in disappointment.

I noticed a man who looked like the blurry face from the picture Hot Boost had texted me walking toward my table. Looking at his attire, I assured myself that it had to be someone else. The guy approaching sported high-top sneakers with no strings, basketball shorts twice his size, an oversized boy band T-shirt, and a camouflage snapback cap. He came to the patio area, looked around, and then went inside. I let out an enormous sigh of relief, and just as the air released from my lungs, my phone rang. The boy band T-shirt guy was exiting the lounge with his phone to his ear. I fumbled with my own phone to turn the ringer off, but I didn't get to it in time. The boy band T-shirt guy walked up and said, "What's up, big head?" It was Hot Boost.

I sunk into my chair in total embarrassment. *You gotta be joking!* I yelled in my head.

"Dang, big head, you look good. Your heels match my hat."

I was wearing camouflage heels. All I could think was, *Who is this man, and where is the real-estate-investing wine connoisseur who reads self-help books I've been talking to for the past three weeks?*

I was waiting for him to tell me it was a prank, but that didn't happen. It was real. Hot Boost was sitting there in the flesh, looking a hot mess. He chewed on a straw while talking to me, and I wanted to slap it from his mouth. *Somebody, help me!* What thirty-something-year-old man shows up to a date like this? I tried to think up a quick ditch plan but told him the truth instead, that I was cold, tired, and ready to go home. I stood up to leave and looked over to gorgeous, sweet-scented Jay. I could only imagine what he was thinking. "Lady, you turned me down for that?"

Hot Boost asked if he could walk with me to my car. "No! No, thank you. I parked across the street. I'll be fine."

"I parked over there too," he said. *Of course he did.*

We walked over to the parking lot and walked by his car first. "This is my baby right here," he said. His car looked like it had been through acid rain.

"Have a good night," I said as I scurried away to my car.

When he drove out of the parking lot, I contemplated going back to the lounge to find Jay, but I was far too embarrassed to face him. I drove away and called my sister. As I explained what had happened, it sounded like a scene out of a romantic comedy. We laughed for my entire thirty-minute drive home.

The next day, as I wrote in my journal and thought back over the prior weeks to pick up any signs missed, I recognized I had given Hot Boost all the information he had needed to impress me. In the first week, I had told him all about my passion for wine and how I was planning a trip to Napa Valley, and I had mentioned the self-help books I was reading. What a coincidence for us to have those specific interests in common—or was it?

Ladies, it's possible to take a seat in the back while sitting in the front row. What I mean is, you can allow the man to take the lead while still being diligent and steering the conversation in the direction you choose. In the rest of this book, I'll show you how.

In my professional career in employee relations, I'm an investigator. My job is to dig for facts. I've developed my own tactful approach to investigating, which mainly involves asking few questions and doing a lot of listening. Once you get people talking, they will voluntarily give you all the information you need. After meeting a few men who weren't who they claimed to be, I began applying my investigative skills to my dating life. My first subject was Dave.

According to Dave's dating app profile, he was a forty-five-year-old gentleman from Louisiana. His Louisiana heritage was apparent from his smooth creole complexion and southern accent. We chatted for one day on the app and exchanged phone numbers. Dave was not a texting man. When I sent him a text message, he took it as an invitation to call me. Since most guys communicated through text messaging 99% of the time, Dave's desire to speak on the phone was refreshing.

Dave jumped right into letting me know he was serious about finding a wife. He had been married once before and was ready to marry again. After we got that conversation out of the way, I shared a few minor details about myself each time we talked and prompted Dave with a general question about himself to get him talking. In one week of listening to Dave talk about himself, I took mental notes of the personal details he shared. Dave was serious about his faith and had developed an organization based on his Christian beliefs. He sent me links to his podcast videos and website, which included a dedication page listing the names of some of his family members and their relation to him. His mother's name was easy to recall because our mothers had the same first name.

Dave was one of the most mature and straightforward men I had met on a dating app in years, but he showed behavior that raised concern in me. During our conversations, he made jokes that I was hinting about wanting to be his wife. I was doing nothing of the sort. He joked about it so often that the jokes felt like a manipulation tactic. I urged him to quit because it made me uncomfortable. He apologized but continued the jokes subtly. It was as if he was trying to put subliminal messages in my head. His behavior seemed red flag-ish and gave off sneaky vibes. Dave was hiding something, and I was going to find it.

Since I was actively dating, I maintained a subscription to a background-check service. For about $20 a month, I ran unlimited background checks. The guys I dated didn't know it, but I entered the name and phone number of every man I chatted with into the background-check system. When I ran the check on Dave, the results generated within fifteen seconds. At first glance, all the information matched up . . . except for one significant discrepancy: the report listed Dave as fifty-five years old instead of forty-five years old, as listed in his profile.

To ensure the information was accurate, I did a mental dump of all the data I had collected from our conversations and compared it to the report. The names of Dave's family members on his website dedication page matched his list of relatives on the report with the proper relation title. His nonprofit organization also showed up on the report. On one of Dave's dating profile pictures, he was standing in front of a house painted a loud blue color with several large plants on the front porch. A Google maps search of the address listed in the report verified it was the same house that appeared in Dave's picture.

If that wasn't enough to convince me, Dave's ex-wife, whose name he had mentioned during a conversation, was listed on the report with the same name. According to the report, she was fifty-two years old.

I called Dave to confront him with my findings. When he answered the call, I went straight to the point.

"How old are you?" I asked.

"Forty-five," he answered.

"When is your birthday?"

Dave told me the exact birthday listed on the report, but the birth year was ten years earlier. "I ordered a background check on you, and your age on the report is fifty-five, not forty-five.

"Well, my friends told me three other guys with my same

name live in northern Louisiana," he explained. "Maybe one of those guys is the fifty-five-year-old."

"Do all of your friends run a background check on you to verify your identity?" I asked. "I'm sure it is you. I saw others too, and not one of them had your same middle name."

Usually, I demanded a FaceTime call within days of meeting someone. I'm unsure how, but Dave had slipped through the cracks for two weeks. I wanted to see his identification, so I called him on FaceTime now. When he came on camera, I could barely see him because he wasn't fully in the camera view, but I saw enough to notice that he looked aged and about fifteen pounds heavier than the person in his profile pictures. He shuffled around as if he was looking for his driver's license, then told me he had left it at home. "Well, show me when you get home," I said.

Dave then turned the focus toward me, as manipulators do. "And you?" he asked. "How do I know you're the person you say you are?"

"I don't doubt you are the person you say you are. I doubt you are the age you said you are."

To weasel his way out of showing me his ID, Dave explained that his home address was on the ID, and he didn't know me well enough to feel comfortable sharing it with me. I told him that the easy fix was to cover his address, but that I already had it on the report. Obviously, he was caught in a lie, and I refused to play the game any longer.

"Look," I said, "if you want to continue talking to me, call me on FaceTime tonight and show me your ID." Dave never called. That experience convinced me that a background check wasn't only the smart thing to do; it was necessary.

If you don't want to pay for a background-check service, free resources are available. You can find a lot of information by conducting a simple internet search. You'll have to enter the information you have in the search box, sometimes in various ways. I ran a Google search using a guy's phone number, and he and his girlfriend's baby registry came up in the search results. Another time, I searched using a guy's name on Google Images. Read this next story to the end to see what I found.

My good friend Will is by far the most social person I know. I often joined him at social events with his friends as a plus-one. At a happy hour event, Will introduced me to PR, and we instantly clicked on a friendly level. PR was a flirt and the life of the party. Over the years, we developed a casual friendship. We only saw each other four or five times a year when I attended events with Will, but PR was my hangout buddy at every event. He constantly flirted, and each time, I gracefully turned down his advances. PR wasn't my type, but he grew on me after four years.

At the time our story takes place, PR and I hadn't seen each other for almost a year, so when he caught my eye at a party Will was throwing, I didn't recognize him until he came over to say hello. He was a few pounds lighter, with longer hair and a less aggressive demeanor than he had had the last time I had seen him. He wasn't as flirty as usual. Though he was still the fun guy, his approach toward me seemed more serious this time. He asked why I was still single five years later, and I responded that I hadn't met the right man yet. Referring to himself, PR pointed out that the right man had been standing in front of me for years. For a second, I considered he could be right. *Had I been looking past a good man for the last five years?* PR wasn't a bad guy, and we had already established a friendship. He deserved a chance, so I gave him one. I imagined it would be a beautiful love story if we ended up together.

There's a difference between knowing someone through

casual conversation and actually *knowing* them. Aside from basic information like his first name, I knew nothing about PR, not even his last name. When I attempted to get to know him on a deeper level, he changed the topic of the conversation to something sexual. It was odd that the man, who appointed himself as the right man for me, did not seem to want to get to know me at all.

For five days, he communicated sporadically in short text messages. He didn't call me once. I had a bad feeling about the situation, but the hope of our fairy-tale romance story playing out was too good to pass up.

I considered asking Will for information, but given that he was friends with both of us, it wouldn't have been fair to put him in the middle of it. PR did some work in the community, so I figured there would be some local photos of him on Google Images. My search resulted in more images of PR than I wanted to see, though.

To my surprise, there was an image of PR standing at a pulpit, preaching. A hyperlink under the image led to a page on PR's church's website displaying a beautiful photo of the assistant pastor—PR—and his wife and kids. This blew my mind.

PR (now known as *Pastor Ratchet* in my mind), the man in the photo with his wife, was the same man making plans for the two of us for Valentine's Day weekend. Seriously, I wondered how he thought this would play out. Though I hadn't involved Will before, I had to confirm that Pastor Ratchet was married. Will confirmed, and I immediately blocked Pastor Ratchet in my phone. I didn't need an explanation because there was nothing he could say to make the situation right. Since then, we haven't been near each other, but I'm sure we'll see each other again someday.

The most significant points I hope you take away from this chapter are to listen more than you speak, be attentive, and give information about yourself in small bits. Most of all, verify that the guy you're talking to is who he says he is. Unfortunately, there are men out there who lie without considering who they might hurt.

In the early stages of dating, the first version of a man you meet will be his representative. You need to get past the representative to get to the real him. You do this by allowing your date to talk about himself. If he doesn't offer up personal information, provide a little about yourself to get the conversation going. Ask questions and make a mental note of every piece of information he gives. Always keep in mind that you are collecting data for your verification check.

If you're actively dating, sign up for a free trial subscription to a background-check service. Once you subscribe, run a check on yourself to see how accurate and updated the company's information is before upgrading to a paid subscription. If, for any reason, you don't want to try a background-check service, run a check on the person you're seeing by entering their name or name and phone number together in a search engine. If you know your date's last name, you can also search for them using their full name on social media platforms. Taking these measures may seem extreme and intrusive, but I assure you it isn't. You have every right to protect yourself from being deceived.

CHAPTER 3

GHOSTING: AN INEVITABLE ONLINE DATING EXPERIENCE

Have you heard the saying "The grass isn't always greener on the other side?" Well, nobody told that to the men on dating apps. Men will ghost you at the drop of a dime. With so many options on dating apps, people are always searching for someone better. According to Statista Research, as of February 8, 2022, there were 44.2 million dating app users in the United States alone, so if you're wondering why that man you met online stopped answering your calls, there you go. Since men can replace you with a quick swipe to the right on the next woman's profile, they see you as easily disposable. I'm willing to bet that anyone who's used a dating app for at least thirty days knows what it feels like to be disposed of or ghosted. I sure do.

Ghosting first reared its ugly head to me through Ditch, my first online date after my divorce. Ditch was a good listener and easy to talk to. After engaging in small talk for two weeks, we planned to meet for a date. It's normal to be nervous about a first date, but this was my first date in sixteen years, so I was having an all-out anxiety attack. On date night, I changed my outfit four times. You know how we do, ladies; we try on multiple outfits and usually land back on that first one. With one hour left to make it to the restaurant, I threw on my black leggings, a white top, and black ankle boots. Before running out the door, I grabbed my bag and sprayed myself with a floral perfume. If my outfit didn't slay, at least I would smell good.

As I drove to the restaurant, my nerves got the best of me. Sweat beads formed on my head, and my hands were shaky. I couldn't stop thinking, *What if he doesn't like me?*

Ditch was standing near his white BMW waiting for me when I arrived. He wore a navy blazer, light blue jeans, and camel-colored shoes. Though he listed his height as six feet in his bio, he was more like five foot nine.

I got out of my car and walked over to Ditch.

"You look nice," he complimented.

"Thanks. You too."

Ditch extended his arm and escorted me into the restaurant. He continued to compliment me on my appearance and said I looked exactly like my profile photos. *Wow!* To be told you look like your photos is the highest compliment you can receive from an online date.

We settled into our booth and the server came over and took our order for drinks and appetizers. Within five minutes of placing our order, though, Ditch received an emergency phone call. After the call ended, he said, "I am so sorry, but I have to leave. My son is with his mom tonight, and she just fell down a flight of stairs."

"That's awful," I said. "Please go!"

As Ditch gathered his phone and wallet from the table, he thanked me for understanding and offered to pay the check if I wanted to stay. "Umm, no, thank you," I murmured. I told him I would stay behind and find the server to cancel the order.

For someone who had gotten an emergency call, Ditch did not seem to be in a hurry at all. He slowly inched his way out of the booth, then strolled leisurely out of the restaurant. Something didn't seem right.

On my drive home, I wondered, *Was there an accident, or did he ditch me?* The next day, I sent him a text message asking if everything was okay. Three days later, he responded, "Hi, sweetheart. Sorry I had to leave." Again, I asked if everything was okay, but this time, he never responded. That was it. I never heard from him again.

I'll admit it, I was naive, but it was odd to me that a forty-year-old man could not simply say, "I'm not interested" or "We're not a good match." Feedback can be tough, whether you're on the giving end or receiving end, but disappearing to avoid having a tough conversation is disrespectful and inconsiderate. It's also downright immature.

I was ghosted a few more times, and some guys had the nerve to come back as if nothing had happened. I wondered if they came back because they felt guilty or because they found out the grass was not greener on the other side. Men ghost because they lose interest or find someone else. They resurface when they get bored or dumped or realize they left a good woman. Ghosters show up weeks or months later to revive what you have already put to rest. There is no acceptable reason to disappear on someone. Any time a man ghosted me and returned, I asked him to answer two questions: Were you abducted, and were you in a coma? If the answer to both is no, we have nothing to discuss.

When I met Casper, he immediately disclosed that he lived in a state hundreds of miles away. He had set his dating profile to reflect the city I lived in because he was moving there in four weeks. Long-distance relationships were not for me, but this seemed like an excellent opportunity to get to know each other from afar.

Over three weeks, Casper and I seemed to vibe well. We had FaceTime calls every night, and he texted me spiritual quotes every morning. Most men I conversed with offline that year texted me morning quotes. Either men think texting morning quotes is the way to a woman's heart, or I really came off to these guys as needing some motivation.

Casper had plans to come to the city to visit his new office and to finalize the lease on his apartment. He added a date with me to his agenda. According to the plan, he would arrive on Thursday morning, handle his business through Friday afternoon, and meet with me for dinner on Friday evening. He arrived on Thursday as planned and called me on FaceTime from the hotel as he was settling in. In the camera view, he began undressing. He took off his shirt, then went for the belt on his pants.

"Whoa!" I yelled. "Can you step outside of the camera view, please?"

"Haven't you seen a naked man before?" he asked.

"Of course I have, but I don't want to see you. We're not there yet."

I figured welcoming the sight of his naked body would give him the idea that I was comfortable being physically intimate with him, and I was not. Casper had somewhat of an attitude about it. He asked, "After three weeks, you're not ready to go to the next level?" I told him that my idea of the next level did not include sex. We hadn't seen if there was any chemistry for us in person yet.

In a cranky tone, he asked, "How long are you expecting me to wait?" The conversation was going all the way left. Don't get me wrong, you should discuss sex with the person you date to make sure you know where you both stand, but discussing it like this would not be productive. Casper was unwilling to hear me out because it had offended him that I had started the conversation by asking him to move out of the camera's view.

He cut off the conversation and said he'd talk to me the next day.

The following morning started off unusually. Casper didn't send me the morning quote. He had never missed a day before, but I thought nothing of it. I assumed he was busy. At around 2:00 p.m., I called to check in, but he didn't pick up. I sent a text message asking him to contact me to confirm our date, but he didn't respond. When 7:00 p.m. came around and my calls were being sent to voice mail, I knew what was going on. There would not be a date. Once he realized we would not be having sex soon, ole boy was done.

What is your first thought when someone you've communicated with regularly suddenly disappears? For most people, the first thought that comes to mind is, "I hope the person is okay." They don't instantly think they were ghosted. I was genuinely concerned about Casper for a few days, but after a week, I finally accepted that I had been ghosted. Again.

After three weeks of silence, I received a text message from Casper: "Hey. Can I call you?" Obviously, he knew I did not welcome a call from him, since he had never requested permission before. "First, answer these questions," I replied. "Were you in a coma? Were you abducted?"

"Huh?" he asked.

That's what I thought.

Of course, the answer to both questions was *no.*

Casper apologized and said he had had a stomach virus and didn't want me to catch it. *Lord have mercy!* The excuses these men come up with are ridiculous. I guess he had had a stomach virus that had disabled his fingers from texting and muted his voice from speaking. I told him to lose my number.

As I said before, ghosters ghost because they lost interest or found someone else. And remember, they come back when they get bored, dumped, or realize they lost a good woman. I didn't know why he ghosted and came back, but I was crystal clear that it was disrespectful, and I had zero tolerance for it.

Ghosting is rejection that blindsides you when you think things are going well. Dating apps have installed this idea of swiping a person away in our minds. They've caused us to see potential dates as just profile pictures, not human beings with actual feelings. There's no consideration of how the other person would process the rejection of being ghosted.

There's one last ghoster I want to tell you about. I call him Tre because he ghosted me three times.

The first time Tre swiped right on my profile, I took a minute to read his bio. He wrote he was a respected educator, a strong leader, a provider, and a God-fearing man who wanted a woman who valued those qualities. I appreciated those qualities in a man, so I swiped right to match with him.

After I sent the first message, Tre responded almost immediately, and we chatted for two days. On the third day, mid-conversation, his profile disappeared. We were unmatched. Our conversation had been going well, so I thought it had to have been a mistake. Two months later, Tre swiped right on my profile again. I matched with him again to give him the opportunity to explain what had happened. I sent the first message, and the next day, he unmatched without ever responding. After that, I knew it had been intentional.

Three months later, Tre swiped right on my profile again. Something was wrong with this man! All but one of my profile pictures were the same, so he had to know it was me. This time, I was curious to find out if he was crazy enough to unmatch me again, so I swiped right and started the conversation. Within seconds, he unmatched. He was playing a weird, childish game, and I was done.

A month later, the most bizarre thing happened. I went to

the gym to meet with my trainer on a day outside of our usual schedule. You will never believe who was in our training area. *Yes!* It was Tre. He was there working with his own trainer. We locked eyes briefly, and I saw the shock come over him. Oh, he knew exactly who he was looking at: the woman he had been playing online hide-and-seek with. He could no longer dehumanize me down to a profile photo. I was a real live person in the flesh.

For a split second, a petty thought came over me. I could approach him and say, "Hey, buddy. Do you remember me?" But it wasn't worth it. Watching Tre staring and putting his head down when I looked his way was much more satisfying. To see my ghoster embarrassed and processing the fact that I was a real person further enhanced my satisfaction.

If nothing else, understand this one thing about being ghosted: You'll never know the real reason a person ghosted you. It's normal to assess your last few interactions with a ghoster to determine whether you said or did anything that would've caused them to go away, but don't linger on it for too long. And definitely do not call or text multiple times a day hoping to get a response, send nasty messages about how terrible of a person they are for ghosting you, or stalk their social media accounts. These behaviors will give them validation that they did the right thing by ghosting you.

When you're serious about finding a partner, getting hopeful and then having that hope stripped away multiple times can take an emotional toll on you. It makes you want to give up trying. If you ever feel this way on your dating journey, don't give up. Take a break from dating to reset, then hop back on when you're ready.

CHAPTER 4

SITUATIONSHIPS: DATING
UNAVAILABLE MEN

My dad is a true southerner who speaks in quotes. He randomly makes them up like they're proverbs from the Bible. One of these quotes is "There's a whole man, a half of a man, and a piece of a man." This has two meanings that depend on the context of the conversation. One refers to the man's character, and the other refers to how much of himself he's willing to give to a woman. In whichever reference it is used, my dad always follows by telling me, "Baby, you deserve a whole man." He also says, "There's a fool, a damn fool, and a goddamn fool. Don't be none of them."

Twice in my dating journey, I did the exact opposite of what my dad said not to do. I was a damn fool who settled for a piece of a man. How did this happen? I didn't have any real expectations in dating, except for wanting a relationship. I believed men's needs were more important than my own and when I was involved with someone, I saw myself as privileged to be with that person. Yep, my thinking was messed up. I'll explain more in chapter six. This mindset caused me to accept unacceptable treatment.

You can tell if you're just getting a piece of a man from how often he texts, calls, and spends time with you. When you're just getting a piece of a man, dates seem more like hanging out and are usually at your place or his. Plans are spontaneous, likely because his other plans fell through. A man who behaves this way does not plan to give you any more than a small piece of himself, but he enjoys having all of you.

Does this sound like anything you've experienced? You may have had a piece of a man and not known it until now. I'll tell you about the tiny piece of a man I held onto for two and a half years.

Late one night, as I was browsing on a dating app where Black people meet, I received a message from a guy who called himself Dr. Sexy (though I called him Dr. Ratchet). I took a peek at his profile, and it impressed me. He was a doctor, but he looked like a football player. This man was fine.

"Hello there," I replied.

"How long do you plan to be awake?" he asked.

"That depends on how this conversation goes."

We chatted until 5:00 a.m.. The conversation went so well that we exchanged phone numbers and resumed our conversation off-line the following evening. We communicated regularly, but it faded after two weeks. Dr. Ratchet invited me to meet in person twice, but I declined. This was back when I had first started online dating, so I was uncomfortable meeting right away. He assumed I was not interested, and he stopped calling.

Three months later, as I was browsing again, Dr. Ratchet sent me a message on the app. "Hey, how's it going?"

"Good!" I responded.

A conversation sparked up from there, and again we took our conversation offline and he invited me to meet in person that weekend. This time, I accepted. Excitement built up in the days leading to the weekend. It felt like I was meeting up with an old friend. When I laid eyes on him at the bar, I almost shouted, *"Yes, honey!"* He was finer in person. I almost tripped over my own feet trying to hurry and get to him. Dr. Ratchet stood five foot eleven, dressed clean, and had beautiful curly hair and manicured fingernails. We talked, laughed, and flirted a lot. Finally, I had a first date that ended well and led to a second.

Dr. Ratchet and I continued seeing each other. A couple of weeks later, we met for dinner. We ended up finding a favorite restaurant where we often met up at the bar, ending the night at his place.

Since I stayed over a couple of nights a week, he requested I write down my favorite body soap and lotion for him so he could have it on hand when I came over. I took that as a sign that he was ready to move the relationship forward. Almost three months had passed, and we had not yet defined the relationship. But, given that we had been spending so much time together, I assumed we were together. I was so clueless about dating rules back then; it is embarrassing.

The next time I went to Dr. Ratchet's place, I asked him, "Where is our relationship going?"

"Relationship?" he inquired.

"That thing we have been doing for the last three months," I reminded him.

"You mean hanging out? I'm not ready for a relationship right now."

"Excuse me! When will you be ready?"

"Maybe at the beginning of the summer," he answered.

It was February! I could not believe what I was hearing. I immediately grabbed my things and left.

When I got home, I called Dr. Ratchet and told him I could not see him anymore since we were not working toward a relationship. "Okay," he mumbled. He acted as if he had never cared at all. It hurt me. I thought, *I am a good woman. How could he just walk away like that?* So ratchet!

Ladies, assume nothing! In relationships, assumptions are setups for disappointment.

I moved on and reactivated my dating app accounts. Days later, I met Jake. He approached me with a joke. Though I can't recall the joke itself, I remember it was a good one. Jake was an average guy with an illuminating smile. His two teenage boys were the same age as mine, and they went to the same school. We had similar careers and family life in common. We immediately hit it off and met in person four days later.

Jake seemed intentional in every area of his life and often talked about his business and his desire to be married. He moved at my pace and never pressured me for physical intimacy. By the time Jake and I had been dating for almost two months, we had not even kissed. On our third date, he had leaned in, but I was not yet comfortable getting that close. A small part of me was still getting over Dr. Ratchet.

Since Jake and I both worked remotely, we met at a local coffee shop at least two days a week to work together. Some days were more productive than others. We did more talking than working. Things were going well. We were building a good romantic foundation, and I had finally moved past Dr. Ratchet.

One afternoon, at one of our work meetings, something magical happened. Jake and I met at the coffee shop earlier in the day than usual and stayed later. While we talked and laughed, an awkward moment transpired where we smiled and stared into each other's eyes. It gave me butterflies. At that moment, I felt feelings turn on inside of me.

We finished our lunch, grabbed our laptops, and walked through the parking lot. When we arrived at my car, Jake smiled and said, "I like you, and I would love for you to consider a serious relationship with me." Then his facial expression turned somber. "But I have to tell you something first."

"Jake, do not tell me you are married. I knew this was too good to be true."

"Please, calm down and have a seat in your car." He took a deep breath and said, "I have a sexually transmitted disease that I will live with for the rest of my life."

My body went numb. I could not speak, and if I could have, I would have had no words to say. He was explaining, but I could hear nothing he was saying. The last thing I heard him say was, "I can understand if you never want to see me again."

The situation was beyond uncomfortable. I told him I needed to process what he had just handed me. *This was heavy.* I felt as if I had gotten the wind knocked out of me. I closed my car door and drove home in silence.

Even today, it is a mystery how I made it home. All I could recall was leaving the parking lot, then pulling into my garage. I walked straight to my bedroom, threw myself on the bed, and cried out to God. "Why? Why does this keep happening to me? Why allow us to get this far, knowing nothing would come of it?" I would rather have not met Jake at all. "Why, God? What did I do so bad in my life to deserve this? Whatever I did, I'm sorry!" I cried myself to sleep that night.

When I woke up the following day, I still could not find the words to speak to Jake. But I would never have to say anything. Our conversation in the parking lot was our last. He never called me, and I never called him. Maybe my reaction had been all he had needed to know it was the end.

The disappointment and sadness I felt were overwhelming. I was tired of losing. And I had thought for sure that Jake would be the guy to sweep me off my feet. I kept thinking about that moment when we had smiled and stared into each other's eyes. It had felt promising. Then, minutes later, it had been snatched away from me. I was resilient, but damn. My heart could only take so much.

This time, instead of hopping back on dating apps, I took time to gather myself and recover. But my recovery period would not last as long as I had expected.

About a month into recovery, a friend invited me to join a girls' night at the club. She knew I had been in the house sulking and thought it would be a good idea for me to get out and have some fun. Though it was "the hood club," I went, and I had a crazy time. It was exactly what I needed to pull me out of my funk. As I drove home, laughing and recalling how my friend kept pointing out a girl's lopsided butt pads, I received a text message. It was from Dr. Ratchet.

"Hey, stranger."

This caught me by surprise. I wondered, *I moved on from him months ago. What does he want?* Rather than acknowledging my fragile state and ignoring the message, I texted back, "Hey there."

Dr. Ratchet was a smooth talker. He responded, "As I sat in our favorite restaurant today, I thought about you."

"Oh," I replied.

"I've missed you. Can I see you tomorrow?" he asked.

Something inside of me screamed, "Nooooo!" But I ignored it. I agreed to see him.

The next day, we met at our favorite restaurant. When I saw Dr. Ratchet sitting at the bar, it was like seeing him for the first time again. I paused and gathered myself together before walking over to my seat next to him. He stood up and greeted me with a hug and a kiss on the cheek. I imagined myself melting into his arms, then snapped back to reality.

"Good to see you," I said.

"You look good," he affirmed.

After finishing our compliments, we updated each other on the last three months of our lives. Eventually, we discussed why things had ended between us and the possibility of picking up where we had left off. Dr. Ratchet expressed that he still was not ready for a relationship, but he could be by the fall. He tried to reel me in with hope, and I took the bait. I made a conscious decision to settle for having a piece of a man, rather than no man at all. I set myself up for a turbulent situationship.

Situationships are undefined relationships. They form when two people function like they are in a relationship, but one individual claims they are not ready to make it an official relationship just yet. That partner has no intention of ever committing, but, in order to keep the other person around, selfishly gives them hope that someday they will. Situationships leave you in a constant state of confusion, wondering where you stand. Why would anyone subject themselves to that? People latch on to situationships for different reasons. They do not believe they deserve more, they're afraid to be alone, or they have a distorted view of love. I latched on for all of those reasons.

Dr. Ratchet and I resumed our noncommitted relationship. I reentered confused and naively believing that we would commit in the fall. Things got off to a good start. Having someone felt good, but the constant confusion of where I stood with him did not. We were not the same as before. It seemed that now he only had time to see me late at night in his bedroom. Any other time, he was too busy. My pride did not let me whine about it though. I had known what I was getting myself back into, but I had not expected that it would make me feel so crappy. This had become an official situationship.

I knew this thing would not last long, but at that stage in

my single life, I just wanted to be in a relationship. It was two weeks shy of fall, and I could not carry on pretending to be okay in an undefined relationship. The word *undefined* hung over my head like a dark cloud.

One evening, after leaving Dr. Ratchet's house, I couldn't escape the feeling that I was selling myself short. The next day, I called to let him know I could not continue how things were. If he still was not ready to commit, I would move on.

Like the last time, he said, "Okay." That was it. He did not ask me to stay or give me some made-up timeline of when he might be ready. Instead, he just repeated, "Okay, I'm sorry you feel that way." I felt hurt and misused. What could I do but move on?

They say the best way to get over a man is to get under a new one. I don't encourage that, but it is precisely what I set out to do. I carried on as if nothing had happened and reactivated my dating app accounts. To be honest, I was trying not to feel because I did not believe the hurt that I felt was valid. It was my fault for being a damn fool and going back to the same man who was in the same state of mind I had left him in when we had last stopped seeing each other. But! My attempt to get under another man halted. I concluded it would only make things worse. Instead, I accepted the negative emotions and gave myself time to process the pain. It was difficult since I had suffered much rejection over the last seven months.

To get my deeper emotions out, I got back into the habit of writing in my journal daily. I was too embarrassed about what I was feeling to talk to anyone but myself and God. I wrote in my journal around eight o'clock every night. One night, I wrote, "What is so wrong with me that Ratchet would let me go, twice?" Within minutes of writing that sentence, I received a text message from Ratchet. He wrote, "Hey you," as if he had not disposed of me like a used tissue a month before.

I told myself, *Nope! Do not respond. Ignore and block him.* Of course, I did not listen. I was not strong enough. He asked if I would meet him for a drink, and while initially I declined, the next day, I gave in. And, just like that, we were back at it.

That would not be the last time Dr. Ratchet and I broke it off and ended up back together. We continued this on-again, off-again cycle for over two years. Here is how it went. We got back together and, at about the two-month mark, guilt and shame got the best of me. I gave Ratchet an ultimatum to either commit or I was done. He rejected my ultimatum, and I broke it off. In between breaks, I dated other people. When I got fed up with bad dates, I returned to Ratchet to repeat the cycle. He welcomed me back with open arms—every time.

One night, as I considered going back to him for the fourth time, I wrote this.

JOURNAL ENTRY

Tonight, I am home relaxing with a bottle of wine and three flaming vanilla candles, listening to Luther and Chrisette radio on Pandora. This music reminds me of how much I want to be in a relationship. I'm sitting here thinking about the last time I was in love and how good it felt.

This friends-with-benefits thing I have with 'Ratchet' is pathetic. I go along with it to have someone when I feel lonely. I hate that he's not a horrible person. He's sweet, caring, and a wonderful dad who is building a good life for his kids. He's even helped me with some personal business. That's why it's so hard to not hope that someday he comes to his senses. The difference in going back this time is that I accepted what he had

*been showing me for the last year. There will never
be a anything real between us. Being ready is not
his issue. He never said it, but I know he does not
want a committed relationship with me. He enjoys
my company, and I enjoy his. Really, I don't even want
a relationship with him anymore. Any man who has
me and won't commit does not see my worth. There
is a man who will not be blind to my value, and I am
leaving my options open to meet him.*

*For now, I am keeping Ratchet around. When I'm
with him, I get to experience the emotion and thrill of
love and connection that I desire, even though it's not
real. And I can't leave out that the sex is amazing. We're
using each other for something we need. It is what it is.*

Acceptance is an excellent state of mind when it is real and
not used to justify an unpleasant situation. I was in denial of
how this situationship was affecting me. Each time I went back
and Dr. Ratchet declined to commit to a serious relationship,
I experienced another level of rejection. Whenever I left his
house knowing he would never see me as more than a fun
sex buddy, I felt more devalued. My false sense of acceptance
twisted my mind to believe I was returning to him on my
terms, and I was in control. That was a lie. Dr. Ratchet was
always in control. There was a reason he would never tell me
he did not want a committed relationship with me. He knew
that if he left me with a tiny window of hope, I would return.

Detaching from Dr. Ratchet was a process. In between
breaks, I blocked his number but unblocked it days later.
I think moving away was my saving grace. I had been job
hunting and landed an interview with one of the biggest
companies in the world. When they called to extend the job

offer, it was for a location in a city three hours away. I hadn't planned to move anytime soon, but there was no way I could turn down that opportunity. At that time, I didn't realize it, but it was perfect timing. After moving away, I had time with myself to reflect and recognize how the situation with Dr. Ratchet really affected me.

I'm not saying you should move hours away to sever a tie, but a little isolation and a lot of prayer worked for me. And then something happened that put the last nail in the coffin.

Five months later, I went back to the city to visit my sister. Out of the blue, Dr. Ratchet sent a text asking when I would be visiting next, as if he knew I was in town. In shock, I called him and asked how he knew I was in town. We didn't have any mutual friends, and he hadn't met my sister.

He asked me to come over to his house for an innocent visit. Then, he said, "Oh, you should know something. I have a girlfriend." I laughed it off. Indeed, he was joking. I don't know why I agreed to visit him, but I found out why I needed to be there when I got there. God has an incredible way of intervening.

As I was heading to the bathroom, I noticed several clear storage containers filled with women's clothing stacked against Dr. Ratchet's bedroom wall. When I asked about the containers, he told me they were for his girlfriend moving in from Georgia. I recalled that when we had first begun seeing each other, he had told me he had recently ended a short-term relationship with a woman in Georgia. It hadn't worked out because distance became an issue. It occurred to me that this was probably the same woman, and he was probably with her throughout our entire situationship. Dr. Ratchet traveled often, so it was possible.

I felt sick, but I was more relieved than hurt. This event gave me the confirmation I had been seeking. Each time Dr.

Ratchet had said he was not ready for a committed relationship, it had been a lie. He had been ready for a relationship—with another woman.

Months later, when I moved back to the city permanently, Dr. Ratchet's girlfriend and her kids were all settled into his home. Regardless, he tried getting back in my bed. He assumed we could pick up where we had left off and that I would, in full awareness, be his side chick. *Hell no!* I smile as I tell you that that did not happen. But his efforts to get me back were confirmation and icing on the cake: he was no good. This opened my eyes to see that God protected me when I made foolish decisions. A serious relationship with Dr. Ratchet would've caused me serious damage.

An emotionally unavailable man will tie your emotions up in a situationship because he knows that he's not equipped for a committed relationship. When Dr. Ratchet tried to get back into my bed, he proved he wasn't fit for a relationship with anyone.

Ladies, grab your journals. If after reading this chapter, you think that your relationship is actually a situationship, answer these questions: Have you been dating for a while, but you find that he avoids or postpones defining the relationship? Does he only make spur of the moment plans to spend time with you? Are your dates usually home dates? Do you feel guilty or ashamed about spending time with him? If you answered yes to two or more of those questions, you're likely in a situationship. Don't feel bad. You're sticking around because you want the guy that you want to want you too. But when you become aware that he doesn't want anything serious with you because he's emotionally unavailable, you have to let go. If you notice that you repeatedly attract unavailable men, consider that a part of you may be unavailable too. I'll discuss this in more detail in chapter six.

CHAPTER 5

PURSUING THE ONE

Most times, when a woman meets a man, she determines she wants him, and she relentlessly tries to convince him she is the one. *Relentlessly.* When he doesn't move at her pace, she becomes anxious and worries that maybe she hasn't shown her worth yet. She then overzealously attempts to prove her value to him. She gives him access to parts of her body and emotions he has not earned and frankly cannot handle. Then she thinks, *Now he'll see how amazing I am.* And, when he doesn't see it, out of desperation, she does more. Sound familiar? Is it you?

Unfortunately, often, that is the way it happens—intentionally or not. So, if you turn the pages of this book and you see yourself in it, please know you are not alone. What we often think is working for us is working against us. More often than not, the more you give absent a committed relationship, the less likely it is that a man will commit. Why? You've heard the old saying, *Why buy the cow when you can get the milk for free,* right? I never liked this saying, but there's some truth to it. If a guy's getting all of the benefits a boyfriend gets before making a commitment, in some guys' minds, there's nothing left to work for. It's also important to remember that, inherently, men are hunters. They want to work for their prize. When we give men the prize without requiring them to put in the work for it, the value of the prize diminishes.

Look at it this way. If a stranger walked up to you and gave you a diamond ring and did not ask for anything in return, wouldn't you think it was fake or that something was wrong with it? That is how men feel when we give them so much of us and they know they have done little to deserve it. They assume something about us is defective. This reminds me . . .

Every time my dad tells the story of how he met his wife he exudes a sense of pride and accomplishment. He smiles like an alligator as he tells his story of chasing her. My dad first laid eyes on his wife as she stood at a bus stop that he drove by every day. Every morning, he slowed down as he approached the bus stop and inched by to get a good glimpse of the mystery woman in her all-white nurse uniform with the cute little hat, but he never stopped to say hello. One day, though, he went to a birthday party at an apartment complex. As he walked up the stairs to get to the party, he saw the mysterious bus-stop woman walking down the stairs. He watched her as she strolled down the walkway and into the apartment next door to the party. *It had to be fate.*

Later, he stepped outside to take a break from the noise and noticed the woman's door was open. He peeked through the open door and watched as the bus-stop woman sat on her couch reading the pages of what he later discovered was her anatomy textbook. She got up and walked toward the door. He spun away, hoping she did not see him staring. She walked outside, and he finally seized the opportunity to get her attention.

"Hello, miss. I'm Albert," he said.

"Tracy," she said.

Albert, *my dad* (proud daughter moment), and Tracy engaged in small talk. Then he offered Tracy his phone and pager number. To his surprise, she took it . . . and he was elated.

Tracy explained that she was a single mom and nursing student with two kids.

"I do not have time for a relationship," she admitted.

"I respect that," he said. "Call me when you're ready."

My dad . . .

My dad knew right then and there that he had a challenge, but he felt one step closer to winning over his dream woman.

One month passed by, and he didn't hear from Tracy. Still, he had hope. Two months later, when he was about to accept that she would not call, she did. Even though he was at a semiformal event at the time, my dad answered. He told Tracy to stand by and that he would call her in ten minutes, and he did. He left his friend's celebratory event to talk to her.

That was the beginning of what later became a twenty-years-and-counting marriage. My dad always ends the story by saying, "That woman wasn't nothing nice. I had to get her. I knew she was the one."

Unashamedly, I wanted a love story like my dad's. I wanted someone who would drop everything when I called two months later because he knew I was the one. For years, I looked for that. Well, "looked for it" is an understatement. I hunted it down. There is no shame in wanting love. All human beings naturally desire love and connection with another person. My problem was that I wanted love to fill a void. I was lonely. I figured if I could just have a man who loved me like my dad loved his wife, it would fulfill me.

One Sunday evening, I checked my dating app subscription to find that I had only five days left as a premium member. Having decided to discontinue my subscription after a series of disastrous dates, I canceled the automatic renewal. I believed God might just send me the one within those five days I had left.

Later that night, I received a message from a guy I had not seen on the app before named Stephan.

"Hi."

Here we go, I thought, *another one here to waste my time. Could he not think of something better to say than "hi"? I am so over this.*

Ignoring the message, I looked at Stephan's profile. It seemed he had put some effort into writing a decent introduction, and he did not have any bathroom selfies, which I always considered a red flag of a narcissistic man. Overall, Stephan's profile was an eight out of ten. He gave off a fun, easygoing vibe. His look was nerdy and did not fit the image of a guy I would usually go for, but my usual choice of men had not served me well so far. It was about time for me to try something new.

In one of his photos, Stephan wore a party mask and did a goofy pose.

"Nice to meet you, Stephan," I replied. "You seem like a fun guy."

"Oh, I try to make the best of every moment," he replied.

We continued our chat, but it was not the ordinary "tell-me-about-yourself" initial interview kind of chat. The conversation flowed with ease. After a few days of pleasantries, we exchanged phone numbers and scheduled a time for a phone call. I felt good about him. Ten minutes before the call, I curled up in my purple velvety chair with a throw blanket and got comfortable. When Stephan called me, the sound of his voice slightly took me by surprise. A nasally, nerdy sound, like an adult Steve Urkel, came through the phone. Mind you, not Stefan Urquelle, the suave alter ego. No, this voice grated on me and immediately brought to mind the *Family Matters* nerd—distinctly unsexy.

"Hello, Stephan. How are you?"

At first, I thought the voice was a sign of nerves, but it did not go away. The conversation was stimulating, but I could not get past the sound of Urkel in my ear. When our call ended, I leaned back in my chair, crossed my arms, and considered, *How can I tell this nice man we are not a good match because he sounds like Steve Urkel?* I felt awfully immature for thinking that, so reserve your judgment. I've already handled it. Moving on.

From one phone conversation, I could tell that Stephan was by far the most decent man I had met in a long time. Yet all I could think about was the absence of sex appeal in his voice. The next day, I told my sister about my reservations with Stephan's voice, and she said, "Stop. You're being silly. Give him a chance." My sister was right, but I still took a few days to think about it. Stephan and I texted throughout the week.

The following Saturday, I went to a play at a downtown theater. It was a boy-meets-girl love story in which the characters replayed scenes with alternative outcomes based on different choices in the same situation. The scenes in the first act convinced me I should give Stephan a chance. They made me think, *What if he is the one, and I make the wrong choice to not meet him because of my pettiness?* I sent him a text message, asking if he could meet me at a nearby café after the play. It was last minute, but fortunately, he was available.

When Stephan arrived at the café, he parked on the opposite side of the parking lot. I watched in the rearview mirror as he got out of his car. He was handsome, of average height, and dressed casually but neatly. I got out of my car and walked over to greet him. As I approached, his eyes scanned me from head to toe. We went inside, ordered drinks, and talked for an hour. Simple. I was so absorbed in our conversation that I did not even notice the sound of Urkel in his voice anymore.

Stephan's personality shined. He was charming, and I was

smitten. We did not expect to meet for long since we both had other plans, so we reluctantly ended our meet and greet. Stephan walked me to my car and asked if he could see me again soon. *Absolutely.* After he drove away, he immediately sent me a text message.

"I enjoyed meeting you. Can't wait to see you again."

After reading the message, I was thankful that I had not foolishly given in to pettiness. The next day, Stephan called and asked me on a date to an upscale patio bar. Four days later, we met for our date.

As I approached the entrance to the bar, I saw him standing there, smiling. He took my hand and escorted me to our seats. Since it was a weekday, we planned to have a drink or two and end the night early, but it did not turn out as planned. Stephan loosened up even more. He had this dorkiness about him that was cute and funny, and he owned it. An hour into our date, a DJ showed up and set up his equipment. He turned the quiet little bar into an all-out party. I cannot be still when groovy music is playing, so naturally, I started dancing. Stephan attempted to dance with me—or do something like dancing. It was hilarious. The music even drew in a crowd from outside, so we had to get comfortably close to each other, but not nearly as close as the couple who were going at it next to us. It was quite an eventful night.

While standing in the restroom line, I had a three-minute conversation with a young lady named Kiana. Kiana was yelling at a lady crying in a restroom stall because she was taking too long. Respectfully, I told Kiana, "The poor girl is crying, so something must be wrong. We don't know what she's going through in there, so instead of yelling at her, let's make sure she's okay." Kiana agreed and apologized to the girl. When the girl finally came out of the stall, she told us her ex-boyfriend was in the club with his new girlfriend, her coworker. *Ouch!*

Twenty minutes later, Kiana found me on the dance floor. She told her friends how I was wise and had calmed her down. Then she bought shots for Stephan and me.

Stephan looked confused. "Do you know her?" he asked.

"Oh, we just had some girl talk in the restroom," I said.

He smiled. "That must have been a hell of a talk. I'd like to hear about it someday."

Despite the fantastic time we were having, we both had to go to work in the morning, so we ended our night. While Stephan walked me to my car, I was floating on a cloud. We arrived and stood there staring at each other for a long moment and then he leaned in for the kiss. *Come and get it!* Well, I didn't say that aloud. Finally, we said our goodbyes and went our separate ways.

Stephan got home before I did. He called and insisted he would stay on the phone until I made it home. We had a deeper discussion about our intentions for dating and what we each desired from a partner. We were each looking for an equal mate with whom to settle down, do life with, and ultimately get married.

As I drove my car into the garage, I thanked Stephan for being my company until I got home, and he asked when I would be available for another date. *Tomorrow!* I thought, but I didn't say that aloud either. My work had recently gotten hectic, so I needed to check my schedule first.

Days later, we went on our second date. Then, we had a third date and a fourth, and after a month and a half, Stephan and I were a thing. We agreed to be exclusive and to give our relationship time to flourish organically. This was unfamiliar territory for me. I had dated no one for longer than a couple of weeks in years. I was enjoying it all. Dating Stephan was the thing I had been waiting for. He was a reliable, generous, attentive, intellectual gentleman who planned actual dates, prioritized me and had his life in order. This had to be the one.

Stephan didn't start as my dream man, but he was different from all the others. He had his stuff together, and from what I could see, the only part missing was a good woman by his side. From the looks of how our relationship was going, I was *the one* for him.

Stephan and I had been dating for three months. He planned dates, took me to nice places, communicated regularly, and was consistent. I know this sounds like ordinary dating, but my dating life had been everything but ordinary, so this was refreshing. My family and friends were excited for me because they hadn't seen me so happy to be with someone in five years. I was also excited but cautious because Stephan and I were exclusive, but not an official couple yet, and I was getting impatient. This arrangement had been Stephan's idea. His reason for wanting to be exclusive, but not official, was that he had been burned in a past relationship, so he wanted to take his time. At the time, I was foolish enough to believe that that made sense. Ladies, if a man tells you he wants to be exclusive, but he's not ready to make the relationship *official* yet, that means he's leaving his options open, but wants you to keep your options closed in case he chooses you.

Can I keep it real with you? *Like, really real?* I turned forty the year I met Stephan. He was a year younger than I was, and his daughter's mom was ten years younger than me. I guess you can say I was a little insecure. I had mixed emotions about being forty. On one hand, I felt fabulous and was prospering in most areas of my life. On the other hand, I couldn't seem to get the thing I wanted most: a relationship. My romantic life was still up in the air. The game changes significantly when you're over forty in the dating world, especially the online dating world. I had this fear that if I turned forty-one and I still wasn't in a relationship, I would end up alone. Since forty-one was coming in four months, I needed Stephan to recognize that I was the one for him—and quickly.

When we had first met, Stephan had told me that he had a two-year old daughter whose mother was all about the drama. Normally, I would shy away from baby-mama drama, but he was honest about it. I could not imagine that someone with as calm a demeanor as Stephan's would be an active participant in the drama. Stephan and his ex had a flexible custody arrangement. The flexible part of it always went in his ex's favor. I have never been the jealous type, but it was evident she had him wrapped around her finger. She didn't show it in the first two months, but maybe that was because she didn't know I existed. I'm not sure if he ever told her about me, but he didn't need to. She knew another woman was in the picture when he had plans every weekend. Suddenly, she called on him for help with personal issues and made last-minute requests to change their parenting schedule, which always caused him inconvenience. He didn't contest because he got more time with his daughter, but it also meant canceling dates with me. I never complained. How could I? He was being a good dad.

As Stephan and I approached the four-month mark, a shift took place in our relationship. He canceled a date because of another last-minute request to switch parenting days, but he invited me over for a date night at home. Our next date was canceled because his ex needed him to take his daughter so she could go on a last-minute trip. Then, a third date was canceled. Our nights out came to a halt. It became routine for me to drive to Stephan's house every Friday evening after work when his days were switched. We both had demanding jobs and would be so exhausted that we'd only spend a couple of hours together before falling asleep. In the morning, I'd leave when the baby woke up. That's how our weekends went moving forward.

Though I spent most Friday nights at Stephan's house, we became distant. I understood he had obligations before we became a part of each other's lives, but he had gotten much too comfortable with me accommodating his life, and he had retreated to lazy dating. In case you've never heard of lazy dating, it's when a man puts forth minimal effort in dating. Stephan and I completely stopped going on dates, and our communication decreased to a few texts a day and a phone call every couple of days. Still, I continued to take the fifty-minute drive to his house every Friday after work as an attempt to show him that I was understanding since I was also a single parent.

On our first date, I had told Stephan I was not interested in a casual relationship or in being friends with benefits. God knows I had had enough of that with Dr. Ratchet. He said he wasn't interested in that either, but it seemed that was the direction we were heading. When I reminded him, he assured me that was not the direction we were going in, but he was still not ready to define our relationship. He gave some excuses about work and how it wasn't a good time to move forward. He never gave me a straightforward answer.

Constantly thinking about where the relationship was going and wondering if he was leading me on gave me anxiety. If I had been being honest with myself, I would've listened to my dad and the voice in my head or discernment telling me a month ago, *Girl, y'all are done.*

One Friday night, I arrived at Stephan's house and pulled into the driveway. My stomach turned sick. At that moment, I knew I wasn't supposed to be there, but going home would take a fifty-minute drive back, and I didn't have it in me. Because of the construction on the road, it had taken me an hour and twenty minutes to get to his house that night. When I walked inside, dead tired from the drive, I had an epiphany. Our balance was off. There was no reciprocity. I had been giving Stephan husband benefits for months when he wasn't even a real boyfriend. He didn't put forth half the effort I did. Why would he if I didn't require it?

We barely spoke that night. I didn't have the strength to discuss our relationship or the lack thereof. I just wanted to get some rest.

The next morning, as I drove away from Stephan's house, I heard a voice in my car say, "You can't do this anymore." I had never heard the audible voice of God, but I am sure that was God speaking to me. "I can't do this anymore," I whispered. "I can't do this anymore." Saying those words gave me a sense of freedom. I was tired. I couldn't do another situationship. If Stephan couldn't commit, I had to let him go.

What happened next can be explained better with a passage I wrote in my journal back then. I want to share this with you so you can see exactly what I was thinking and how I was feeling at that time.

JOURNAL ENTRY

This morning, when I got home from Stephan's house, I sent him a text message telling him how I felt. First, let me say, I can't continue to go to his house on Friday night and leave early Saturday morning when his kid wakes up and be okay with it. Also, I cannot continue being with him without a commitment. We're not progressing. He hasn't introduced me to anyone important to him, and when I asked him to come to dinner with my friend and her husband, he agreed and then suddenly got busy. This didn't sit right with me, but I didn't say anything.

Back to when I got home . . . I sent Stephan a message asking him if he saw our relationship progressing because I wasn't feeling this dwelling phase. I hated being in limbo every day thinking, 'Maybe he's ready today.'

Eight hours later . . . Eight hours later! He responded with a message no woman wants to get from a man: "You're a good woman, but . . ." You know nothing good comes after "but." He said he really liked me, but he wasn't sure if he was ready for a relationship. Really, dude? You had the opportunity to tell me that a month ago when I asked if we were still on the same page and working toward a relationship. Now this? I guess he had been stringing me along.

He went on to say, "I know I'm fortunate to be with you, blah, blah, blah." I was not trying to hear that. Finally, we got on a call, and he was talking that same stuff. His excuse for not wanting a relationship "right now" was that he had been busy with work and being a dad. Basically, he didn't have time to be a good boyfriend. He said he should've been spending more time with me, taking me out, and communicating better, but he wasn't sure he had the capacity to be in a serious relationship. I tried to be understanding, but that was some BS. I just said okay. It's not like I was trying to change his mind. But here's what got me.

I said, "Well, I guess that's it for us." This dude said we were having a good time and asked if we

*could leave things how they were for now. What! I was
offended. Who was having a good time? Not me! He
wanted me to put myself on layaway for him. I told
him that was absolutely not going to happen. Should
I be fine with being in limbo, not knowing where I
stand for the next—what? Two or three months? No!*

*He said, "Well, let's be friends without the
sleepovers. We could still hang out." Oh, now he
has time to hang out. That was just dumb. I don't
want to be his friend. I have enough friends! I want
a relationship!*

During my phone call with Stephan, he repeated multiple times
that he didn't want us to end. I believed he didn't want the benefits
to end, but he did want my expectation of a serious relationship
to end, and it did. There was no way he would get another minute
of my time. I told him we were done, and I meant it.

I have to admit, my situation with Stephan was a bit
confusing. I mean, who agrees to date exclusively but not
define the relationship? I did. And I did it because I so badly
wanted a relationship that I was willing to settle for anything
to get it. I was anxious and, honestly, a little desperate. I saw
Stephan as my last chance for a relationship because I was
tired of online dating. By then, I had been on and off dating
apps for five years, and I dreaded getting back on.

Ladies, don't get so caught up in finding the one that you ignore
all the signs that are showing you he's not the one for you. And
don't allow your desire for a relationship to cloud your thinking
(like I did). I tried to force a relationship that wasn't meant to be.

If, after reading this chapter, you feel that you're currently in
a similar situation to the one I was in, ask yourself why you're
still in it. Grab your journal and answer these questions: Does

the relationship bring you joy or anxiety? What makes you feel good about the relationship? What makes you feel anxious about the relationship? Is it clear that you're in the relationship for the wrong reasons? What are those reasons? Can the relationship possibly be salvaged, or is it clear that you should end it now? How will you proceed with communicating your newfound perspective to the person you're dating?

In the next few chapters, I'll dig deeper into the reasons why we hold on to unhealthy relationships like this one and how to break away from settling for less than we deserve.

PART TWO

THE HEALING JOURNEY

A Mindset Transformation

CHAPTER 6

THE INNER WORK: BREAKING FREE FROM LIMITING BELIEFS

The turn in the relationship with Stephan left me confused. Though I was proud that I'd put myself first and walked away, I still couldn't understand why I was a magnet for unavailable men. I just wanted to find a decent guy and be happy. There's a saying that goes "You don't need a relationship until you don't need a relationship." If you believe, as I did, that once you're in a relationship you will be fulfilled, then you are sadly mistaken. A relationship is not a prerequisite to happiness. Deal with the reasons why you are unhappy before welcoming someone into your life. If you are unhappy alone, that won't change when you become connected to someone—and your reliance on them to make you happy will likely run them away. I was unhappy, and I convinced myself that being in a relationship was the key to my happiness. But I didn't need a man. I needed healing. God had a plan for me, and it did involve a relationship—but with myself.

In the past few years, popular influencers in the self-love and dating space have been empowering women to adopt the queen mindset. It's a mindset of confidence, independence, high self-worth, valuing your mind and body, and embracing your authentic self. I couldn't take it seriously because I struggled to identify. When I looked in the mirror, I didn't see a queen. I saw a reflection of a damaged woman full of guilt, shame, and negative self-beliefs. My relationship with myself was toxic, and I needed to fix it.

One afternoon, after an intense cardio workout, I sluggishly made my way to the bathroom and turned on the shower. When the water warmed up to the perfect temperature, I stepped in, closed my eyes, and let out a deep breath. Suddenly, I lost my footing and slipped onto the shower floor. While attempting to get up, I slipped again and burst into tears.

Physically, I wasn't hurt, but out of nowhere, sadness came down on me hard, and inside, it hurt like hell. I laid there on the shower floor and cried inconsolably to the point that I could barely breathe. If I was physically hurt, there was no bae I could call for help. For the first time, I felt alone. And since I didn't have the strength to suppress my emotions as I usually did, I felt every bit of the loneliness, guilt, shame, anger, and disappointment that had plagued my thoughts and emotions for years. Maybe God grew tired of watching me pretending to be okay, so he stepped in for an intervention.

I pulled myself up from the shower floor—successfully this time—and said, *"Okay, God. I'm tired. I surrender."* That night, I wrote a simple prayer of surrender in my journal.

MY PRAYER OF SURRENDER

"God, today I am making a commitment to surrender to my healing season. Let your Spirit be my guide and comfort on this spiritual journey because I know this is going to be hard. For a long time, I have been avoiding my issues. I just wanted to forget about them. But now I am ready to face them and let go. I need to be free. I need to value myself more, love myself better,

*and truly believe that I deserve love. I have to stop
chasing relationships and ending up with the same
type of man each time. Why do I attract the same
unavailable type? I need answers and insight into
the root of my emotional pain and bad relationship
choices. I commit now to doing the work to heal."*

If you find yourself at a point of surrender, start with a prayer
of your own. If you're not a praying person, speak these simple
words: "I surrender to my season to heal." There's no doubt
healing is hard. I suggest maintaining a journal throughout
your healing process because it will come in handy when you're
tempted to quit. By keeping a journal, I was able to look back
and remind myself of my purpose for healing and how far I've
come in the process.

Self-reflection is crucial in identifying why we feel and
behave the way we do. It's often avoided because it requires
acknowledging painful emotions and being honest with
ourselves about our negative behavior patterns. Before we
can change our behavior, we have to understand what drives it.
In my period of self-reflection, I took a step back from dating
so I could focus on myself. I evaluated my past relationships
and identified patterns in my behavior and decision-making.
A major driver of my negative behaviors was that I defined
myself by my past mistakes, which caused me to believe I did
not deserve good relationships.

I recalled when my ex-husband and I divorced. I didn't allow
myself to grieve. I thought, *Why should I be allowed to grieve
when I am the one who asked for the divorce?* My ex-husband
didn't want a divorce, but I needed it—and yet in the end,
I didn't feel the freedom I expected to feel. I felt guilty for
removing my children's father from our home. Though I didn't

need my ex-husband anymore, I knew my children still needed him, so I felt selfish for putting my needs before theirs. In time, though, I did grow to trust that I had made the right decision. I realized my children would benefit more from a mentally healthy mother than a miserable, depressed mother.

My ex-husband and I had dated for one year before we got married. One year into our marriage, I realized I had married a person I barely knew. I didn't know his actual age until after we were married. I thought he was eight years older than I was, but, after a few months of being married, I found out that he was thirteen years older. Today, I can't confidently say if knowing that before I married him would have made a difference or not.

When we got married, I was a kid who had no idea what a good marriage looked like. At the time, there were no good examples in my family. My ex understood the complexities of marriage since he had been married before, but he still didn't have it all figured out. Neither of us was good at communicating our needs to each other. My attempts to express my needs didn't seem to get through to him. It often led to arguments where he would laugh as if I was a joke, leaving me feeling unappreciated, disrespected, and misunderstood. I didn't know what to do. So, out of frustration, I shut down.

I met someone who listened and empathized with my issues. He had experienced similar problems in his relationship and seemed to know exactly what I was going through. We quickly formed an emotional bond that transitioned into a full-on affair. Months later, my ex-husband discovered the affair when he came across messages exchanged between the other man and me. Honestly, I wasn't doing much to hide it. Since I didn't have the courage to leave the marriage of my own volition, a part of me hoped that he would leave me, but to my surprise, he stayed. As you can imagine, our marriage became even more difficult.

For the duration of our marriage, he used my infidelity against me. He said and did things to spite, manipulate, and punish me. Though he was not perfect during our marriage, I tolerated the treatment. I felt that I deserved it for my actions, but eventually, it became too much. Somehow the marriage lasted another five years before we divorced, but it had been over long before the affair.

After the divorce, I still had not forgiven myself for the affair. I carried a load of shame. I made poor choices in dating and accepted disrespectful treatment from men because I believed I was a bad person who deserved it. When men treated me well, I sabotaged the relationship because, in my mind, they were too good for me. Shame frequently reminded me that I did not deserve love. Consciously, I wanted a loving relationship, but deep down inside, I feared true intimacy. I believed that if I had a good relationship, I would mess it up; therefore, I settled for situationships. I sought out emotionally unavailable men because I was also emotionally unavailable.

To truly believe you deserve love and happiness, you must let go of guilt and shame and forgive yourself for past mistakes. Since I caused pain, I believed I deserved pain, so I subconsciously subjected myself to it. After acknowledging this, I learned to have compassion for myself. Just as I extended grace to others and forgave them, I had to do the same for myself. A common belief is that the purpose of forgiving others is to relieve their guilt. Instead, the purpose of forgiving someone is to free yourself from the pain of their actions and the hold those actions have over you. Forgiveness is all about you.

Admittedly, I struggled with impostor syndrome for most of my life, not only professionally but also in dating and relationships. I held on to a false belief that I would never be enough. Because of this, I didn't show up as my true self with men. I showed up as whomever I believed they needed me to be. When I dated intellectual men, I turned up my intellect. When I dated funny men, I turned up my humor. I showed them the parts of me I was confident they would appreciate and hid the parts I was unsure they would accept. After doing this for so many years, I almost lost touch with my own personality. I didn't know how to be myself around men.

Because of my negative self-beliefs, I believed that certain men were too good for me. When I browsed dating apps and came across the profiles of men who seemed to have achieved high levels of success, I swiped past them. Though I had achieved a good amount of success myself, I knew eventually I would fear they were too good for me. When I did date successful men, I was anxious, wondering daily, *Is today the day he'll realize he's too good for me?* Sounds like torture, right? It was.

Ladies, I was doing well in most areas of my life and believed a relationship was all that I needed to be happy. But, as you can see, I would never be happy in a relationship in the state I was in. I would've continued to repeat cycles of relationship sabotage until I healed from my issues and from the limiting belief that I did not deserve love. This was a complicated issue that I couldn't overcome on my own, so I had to deal with it in therapy.

Relationships aren't the key to happiness; self-love is. Should you ever feel that you need to be in a relationship with anyone, understand that it cannot cure loneliness, depression, or any other unaddressed trauma wounds you may have. Believing your happiness is tied to being attached to someone and the validation they give you may be a sign that there are deeper issues needing to be addressed. Your most important relationship in life is with yourself. You have to know what loving you looks and feels like before you can show someone else how to do it. Believe me, this will make a world of difference in your dating life.

If anything in this chapter resonated with you, take some time to consider if you need your own healing journey, or even therapy if you've identified deep wounds. Are there any limiting beliefs that you're holding on to that are holding you back from loving yourself the right way? What past mistakes are you hanging onto that have caused you to believe you're not deserving of genuine love? Go to a place where you can have quiet, uninterrupted time to yourself and ask yourself these questions and reflect. Have your journal on hand so you can document your answers and how you feel in the moment.

CHAPTER 7

SEX AND DATING:
KNOW YOUR TRIGGERS

As I continued my healing journey, I examined areas of my life that I had not desired to change before. Sex was not something I wanted to address since I didn't plan to set limits for my sexual activity, but since I was being serious about my healing, no area was off-limits. Though I did not want to admit that sex outside of committed relationships was an issue for me, I knew it was. In new relationships, I led with sex because I believed it was the way to get what I wanted most: love. Instead, I got unhealthy emotional attachments, regret, and diminished self-value. When I gained this insight, I committed to practicing abstinence.

Vowing to be abstinent is more than making a declaration to not have sex for a period of time or until marriage. It involves practicing self-control and suppressing desires to avoid situations we may regret later. To be successful at abstaining, we must know our triggers and patterns. A trigger is something that causes a reaction. A pattern is a repetitive behavior or reaction induced by a trigger. If we're not careful, sex can simply become a response to a trigger, instead of a healthy choice. So, what triggers you to get into someone's bed when you know you'll leave worse off than you were when you got there? I'll tell you about my triggers.

LONELINESS

Before I started my healing journey, I was a life-of-the-party type of girl. My friends and family could always count on me to be the entertainment. I would sing, dance, and say and do the silliest things to create a fun vibe for everyone. Most times, I was the only single or uncoupled person in attendance at events, and it didn't faze me. But at the end of each night, when I got home alone, the fact that there was no one to go home to was depressing. I'd think to myself, *What's wrong with me? I'm a good woman, dammit! Why can't a good man see that?*

It was a lonely feeling, and that loneliness triggered me to turn to someone for validation (usually Dr. Ratchet). There were times we didn't speak for weeks, but whenever I sent him a text message after 9:00 p.m. asking, "What u doin?" 99% of the time, he responded, "The door is open." And within fifteen minutes, I would be in his bed.

Being with him in those times wasn't about sexual pleasure. It was about feeling that there was someone who valued me. I placed high value on sex because back then, in my twisted mind, sex was equal to love. But as I mentioned in chapter four, every time I left Dr. Ratchet's house, I felt more and more devalued.

How do you respond when you feel lonely? If you respond to loneliness by seeking validation, it's a sign that a period of abstinence may be beneficial to you.

INSECURITY

After an incredible night filled with live music and dancing, my date drove us back to his place. By the time we made it to the house, we were both exhausted. Since I had spent the night there a couple of times before, I didn't hesitate to go into the bedroom and settle into the far left side of the bed. Shortly after, he got in bed and made his way over to where I was nestled. He leaned in for a kiss and gently caressed my back. I got a bit nervous and assumed he was looking for sex (like guys I dated in the past had). We had only known each other for three weeks, and in the prior month, I had promised myself I would reserve sex for after a commitment so it wouldn't steer my emotions and lead me to end up in another situationship. I moved his hands and explained that I reserved sex for within the bounds of a committed relationship. He was a gentleman about it and moved away with no questions asked and went to sleep. That should have been the end of our night, but it wasn't.

I had expected at least one attempt from him to persuade me otherwise, so his immediate compliance messed with my mind a little. Honestly, I really wanted to go there, but I also needed to set boundaries for myself. So far, it was working. But then my mind went into overload. I had a conversation with myself. *What are you thinking? He likes you and you like him. You finally have a good guy. Now is not the time to get noble. If you don't have sex with this man, you won't see him again.* My insecurity convinced me that, after that night, my date would not see any value in me if I didn't give him what I had tricked myself into believing he wanted, so I woke him up to have sex.

I wish I could give him credit for doing some clever psychology on me, but I can't. I did it to myself. I allowed my own mind to get the best of me.

SPIRITUAL BONDS

Soul ties are deep spiritual bonds that develop in relationships built on anything but love. You'll know you have a soul tie with a man when his treatment toward you is disrespectful, but you can't resist him. You might conjure up enough strength to let him go, but you won't have the strength to not let him back in when he returns. You'll be frustrated with yourself for not knowing why you cannot keep him out of your life. The frustration will then lead to guilt from devaluing yourself. You're left in a state of confusion as he's out enjoying his life, unconcerned about you.

I know this because my nearly three-year situationship with Dr. Ratchet was sustained by a soul tie. From the beginning, we formed a sexual bond. At some point, I didn't even like him anymore, but I kept going back. The year before I moved three hours away from him, I decided I had had enough. For twelve months, I resisted letting him back into my life. It was tough when he checked in every couple of months, but I stood fast to my decision.

In month thirteen, I experienced what I believe was a spiritual invasion by this soul tie. I was being drawn back to Dr. Ratchet like Neo to the Matrix and was wrestling with getting him out of my thoughts. My big sister was my accountability partner. Without her and a lot of prayers, I never would've been strong enough to resist the urge to call him and reject his advances for an entire year. She kept me in check and reminded me that I deserved better.

When I was finally drawn back, I didn't tell my sister what was going on because I was ready to give in. The need to feel desired was overtaking me. I knew that if he checked in before I could get past my period of weakness, I would entertain his advances. Sure enough, he called, and I agreed to meet with him. A couple of days later, I was back in his bed. Twelve months of victory went down the drain. It wasn't all a waste, though, because I saw that it was possible to break away from a soul tie. I just needed to figure out how to sever the tie for good.

During my healing journey, I ultimately was able to sever

the tie. A major part of that victory was doing the inner work described in chapter six. As I did the work, my self-love overpowered the need for outside validation. I realized everything I needed was already within me.

ENTERTAINMENT

Music invokes lots of emotions, both good and bad. Our favorite songs are usually the ones that remind us of our best and worst memories and cause us to recall events, feelings, scents, touch, and sounds. I love '90s R&B slow jams. Most songs are the perfect mix of sexy and sensual without becoming too explicit. In my early stage of practicing abstinence, I could not listen to those songs because many of them were on playlists I had made specifically for getting in the mood—and don't act like you never had one of those playlists. They're made to heighten the sexual mood, so naturally, the songs were triggers for sexual cravings.

Let's talk about highly sexual movies. Yes, I had to go there. I didn't specify pornography because these days, even made-for-TV movies can be highly sexual. When I began practicing abstinence, I figured watching sex-filled movies would be a safe way to satisfy sexual cravings. At least I wasn't sleeping with anyone, right? Wrong! It temporarily fulfilled my sexual desire, continuously fed the lust, and I ended up at square one more times than I'd like to admit. Sex-filled movies will not make abstaining easier. On the contrary, watching them makes lust stronger and weakens your self-discipline. In tempting situations, it will be harder to maintain control.

In assessing myself, I found my choices of music and movies to play a part in my inability to successfully practice abstinence. Even today, I maintain awareness of the amount of certain music I listen to and the movies I watch. It may seem like a bit much, but I know myself enough to know how much I can take before I get overtaken by mood and emotions. Do the movies you watch invoke sexual desires in you, or does the music you listen to? Has either driven your decisions concerning sex? If you answered yes to either of those questions, consider excluding those movies and songs from your entertainment altogether for a period of time. Then introduce them back slowly so you can gauge how much you can handle.

PUTTING IT INTO PRACTICE

I took a break from dating for six months when I started practicing abstinence, and, at that point, I hadn't been intimate with anyone for the six months prior. When I was ready to date again, I went back to online dating, but it was quite different this time.

Meet Johnny. He was a fun guy with a good balance of dorkiness and swag. We talked on FaceTime every other night for two weeks. Johnny and I shared stories like we were old friends. I felt like I had a good prospect right out of the gate.

One night, on a FaceTime call, Johnny cleared his throat and asked, "When was the last time your oil was changed?"

"Why? Do you want to change it for me?"

He laughed and clarified. "Not in your car; think about it."

"Ohhhh," I said. "Are you asking about the last time I had sex?"

"Well, when you put it that way," he said.

"No, you put it that way," I said. "That's not important, but if you must know, it's been a year."

"A year! Are you practicing to become a nun?"

"Lord have mercy," I said. "Tell me how you really feel."

He laughed and said he was playing, but I knew what time it was. Johnny's reaction was priceless, and it made his intentions crystal clear to me. The fact that he wanted to know the last time I had had sex was a red flag, but I wanted to give him a chance to explain. Suddenly, though, he needed to end the call because he had business to handle.

That was our last conversation. I never heard from Johnny again. And I never called him back.

Look, I know this chapter will not be for everyone. I shared these stories with you because I know I'm not the only woman who has made decisions I regret regarding sex. On the surface, you may see sex as just a physical act, but if you feel any regret after the act, consider that there may be a deeper issue that needs to be addressed. Think back on any time you ended up in someone's bed and regretted it. Look to identify common triggers and responses.

Practicing abstinence gave me a higher sense of value for my body and my overall self. This perspective helped me to change how I approach the subject of sex in new relationships and to establish healthier boundaries around sex.

You may not have any interest in abstaining from sex. I get it. But I implore you to be open to it if you have any conviction or curiosity after reading this chapter.

CHAPTER 8

ME-TIME: RECONNECTING
BACK TO SELF

In earlier chapters, I discussed how I hid my true self to appeal to men and, in doing so, nearly lost touch with who I was. My willingness to change for others was an indication that I did not truly like myself, and I'll admit, I didn't like much of the person that turned me into. I was anxious, needy, insecure, and desperate for love.

Losing my sense of identity started long before I began online dating. When I married my much older ex-husband at twenty-one, I was naive and vulnerable to being shaped and molded. Throughout our marriage, I became much of who he wanted me to be and slowly shed parts of my identity. He didn't like certain clothes I wore, so I changed my style. I was social, but he was a loner. He often said I was friendly and fun with everyone but him, so I toned down the social side of me. In the final years of the marriage, I reclaimed some parts of myself, but after the divorce, I resumed my people-pleasing ways that I'm sure I developed somewhere in my teenage years. During my healing journey, I realized how my toxic need for acceptance and validation drove me to pretend to be someone I was not. It was confusing and exhausting.

To reconnect with my authentic self, I embarked on a mission of self-discovery. I needed to build a relationship with myself before I could have one with anyone else. To build a relationship with yourself, you have to spend time with yourself. It's the same as building a relationship with someone new. You won't discover those small things you appreciate about them unless you spend quality time together.

So, how do you reach a place where you are comfortable spending quality time alone? First, know that being alone and being lonely are not the same. You've probably heard many times before that when you learn how to be alone, you will never be lonely again. It's true. When you become your own best friend, you'll learn to appreciate how awesome you are, and you'll realize that spending time with you is a privilege not to be taken for granted.

I had a friend, Damon, who had lots of lady friends. He hated being alone. Whenever he felt lonely, he texted his lady friends to find one who was available to spend the night with him. If none were available, he logged on to a dating site to find someone to chat with. Ladies, guys like Damon are why you have a great conversation with a guy one day and never hear from him again. He was simply there for entertainment, nothing more.

One day, I asked Damon why he had different women in his bed throughout the week. He said he hated being alone with his thoughts. There were likely some issues he needed to address in therapy. Before, I had thought Damon had so many women because he was greedy, but that wasn't completely the case. It was because the women were his avoidance mechanism—*and* he also was greedy. But I felt bad for my friend. He constantly needed to have someone around to help him escape from himself.

I told you Damon's story because I want you to see why the inner work has to be done in order to successfully connect with yourself. If you don't take the time to heal and deal with the things that eat at you, it'll be difficult for you to believe you're worth spending time with at all, let alone to think that time with you can be enjoyable.

Many times, I skipped out on an event or getting out of the house on the weekend because I didn't have anyone to join me. The thought of going alone to a place where people would typically go to hang out with friends felt awkward. I found eating alone at restaurants to be the most intimidating. Have you ever seen anyone dining alone? I have, and I assumed that person was lonely. Now, though, I feel like an idiot for assuming that. I should've been thinking about how I could get myself to a place where I'd be bold enough to sit at a table for one.

To chow down at a table alone in a restaurant full of people without feeling awkward, you have to really enjoy your own company. I wanted to be that bold and content in my own company, so one afternoon, after leaving the mall, I decided to stop at a restaurant where I often got crab cakes with friends.

When I pulled my car into the restaurant parking lot, I got nervous. I wasn't ready. I walked up to the entrance and stood outside for five minutes, then turned around and went back to my car. I was terrified. I sat in my car and listened to music until I built up enough courage to try again. I walked back to the entrance, but I couldn't go inside. I got back in my car and drove away. The hostess must've thought I was a crazy stalker person. As I drove away, I justified not following through by telling myself that normal people don't dine alone. I felt like a coward, and I really wanted those crab cakes, so I made a U-turn and went back.

This time, I went inside and sat at the bar. I felt like everyone was staring at me. It was an uncomfortable feeling, but I stuck it out. The bartender came over to take my order, asked how my day was going, and stuck around to talk. That was the perfect opportunity to ease me into this. We talked for almost my entire time at the restaurant, when he wasn't making drinks. Thank God for chatty bartenders.

I ended up going to that same restaurant once a week and chatting with my favorite bartender. When he wasn't working, I put my earbuds in to listen to music and immerse myself in my own world. Soon, I stopped escaping into music or books when I dined alone and got comfortable enough to take my earbuds out and strike up conversations with strangers. I became a pro conversation starter. But when I didn't feel like talking to people, I left my earbuds in. It worked most of the time, but there was always that one person who talked to me anyway.

After getting past the awkwardness of being in social settings alone, I felt comfortable and empowered to do more. I never missed another event or had another weekend at home wishing I had someone to go out with.

If you've never tried doing anything alone, you have to give it a try. It's a freeing experience to be able to enjoy your own company while being surrounded by people. They might stare at you, but not because you're awkward—because they admire your freedom.

In my attempts to reconnect with my social side, I joined Meetup groups and attended networking events to hopefully meet some new connections and girlfriends. There was one group of ladies I met on Meetup who was wild and free and exactly the excitement I needed. We had dinner parties, live music nights, and wine tastings every month. The events were a blast, and sometimes things got a little out of control, but it was all in good spirits.

One of the ladies had a passion party at her house. I had never been to a passion party, so I was excited about the experience. For those of you who don't know what a passion party is,

I'll explain. It's like a Tupperware party. A group of women get together, play games, and celebrate being women. But the difference is that we shop for sex toys and products that create a more sensual environment for the bedroom.

When I arrived at the party, the hostess took me to her home office, where the adult items were displayed. I shopped around but, since I was not participating in activities wherein I could utilize those items, I purchased a soy candle. After the purchase, we retreated to the living room to join the other ladies playing a game of truth or dare. Midway through the game, the hostess's husband walked up and whispered something in his wife's ear that got her excited, and then he left the house. With a wide smile, she whispered, "My husband is going to get our unicorn." The ladies all looked at each other in confusion. The hostess was so excited that she ended the game, turned on music, and began exotic dancing. That was when the weirdness started.

Thirty minutes after the husband left the house, a man rang the doorbell. When the hostess opened the door, he came in and walked directly over to a friend of the hostess and wrapped his arms around her. They started dancing and got closer and closer. I thought I was watching the Black version of *Dirty Dancing*. I wanted to yell, "Go into a room already!" It was evident that they wanted to do more than dancing.

The husband arrived back home with a fine, younger, handsome man. One of the ladies, Sheba, leaned over to me and whispered, "There's the unicorn."

I said, "Damn girl, I want one."

The men joined the ladies in the living room, and it quickly began to feel like everyone knew each other except for me and Sheba. They were all laughing, dancing, and touching each other. I still didn't know what the unicorn reference meant, so I asked Sheba. She informed me that a unicorn is an individual who is single, enjoys pleasing the husband and wife, and enjoys the swinging lifestyle. The hostess and her husband were swingers. It finally clicked in my head that this passion party was soon going to turn into a swinging party. It was time for me to go.

I looked for the hostess to thank her for her hospitality, but she was nowhere to be found. Suddenly, she burst out of nowhere in a silky robe. She flashed it open to expose her lacy lingerie and said, "I hope y'all are ready for this." While I stood there frozen, the dirty dancers started dropping their pants. I had never seen anything like this in my life.

Sheba turned to the husband and asked if she could stay and watch. The husband said, "Only if you get naked." She grabbed my hand and we raced to the door and got out of there. I laughed in shock the entire ride home. Though I hadn't stuck around for the events that I assume were about to take place, I had still had a good time with those ladies and the ladies' group overall. I met some good women, none of whom I'm friends with today, but still, the group was a great way for me to get comfortable with being social and meeting new people.

If you're looking to have a more robust social life and you don't have a large circle of friends, I recommend trying Meetup. It's a community social networking platform that hosts organized groups where people come together to meet others with similar interests. Group facilitators put together virtual and in-person events to take part in. Sound interesting? Give it a try.

Continuing in the spirit of trying new things, I signed my eleven-year-old son up for the community soccer team. I figured it was a new experience we could try together. Two days before the first practice, the coach quit the team. Guess who was asked to step in and coach? *Yep!* It was me. At the time, I was in the Army Reserves, and I had mentioned that to one of the moms in small talk. She had told the other moms and, based on that piece of information, they collectively decided that my leadership skills qualified me to coach soccer.

Now, there were parents whose kids had played for years. They had to know more about soccer than I did. I hadn't seen or played one game of soccer, ever. But in the spirit of trying new things, I did it. I coached a community soccer team.

This may not seem like a huge deal, but it was for me. Coaching soccer was not something I had ever considered. I never even watched the sport, so I didn't know the rules, and neither did my son. I made the wrong calls, and my son kicked the ball in the wrong direction more than once. We only won two games, but the overall experience was rewarding. When the season was over, my son retired his number two jersey, and I retired my coach whistle.

Today, I don't completely know why those parents didn't choose someone who actually knew the rules of soccer, but I'm glad they chose me. It turned out to be the perfect opportunity to step outside of my comfort zone, and it was quite gratifying. We'll all make it to a level of comfort where we can navigate life on autopilot. But think about it: Does having your life on autopilot challenge you to do more and become an even better version of the awesome person you are now? What can you do in the next week to step outside your comfort zone and experience something new? Don't just think about it, do it.

As my connection to myself grew stronger, so did my confidence and drive to improve my life overall. I thought about what my ideal life looked like, and I realized it was the perfect time to work on the details and set goals. In my ideal life, I would achieve an MBA in human resources, progress in my career, earn a comfortable salary with disposable income, start my own business, and buy a beautiful home. To get started, I wrote down my goals in a journal, established a timeline for completion, drafted detailed actions to take to accomplish each goal, and got to work. Within the first two years, I achieved my first two goals, and in the next year and a half, I completed the others, with some residuals along the way.

You may be asking why I'm mentioning goals. Well, when you reconnect with yourself, you get a sense of empowerment and belief that you're worthy of having your ideal life. It's the perfect time to work toward the things you've been procrastinating on because you didn't feel like you deserved them.

What does your ideal life look like? Grab your journal and write your answer to this question, and then work backward from there. Write down at least three tangible things you'd like to accomplish. You may see yourself ten pounds lighter with your own business in a new home. Write the steps you will take to accomplish those things and lay out a timeline for completion. Now, what are your intangible goals? You may see yourself as more comfortable in social settings, or you may imagine yourself trying new activities. Detailed goal-setting isn't the easiest thing to do. If you need guidance, visit my website, seanmariebee.com/freebies/, and download the SMART Goals Workbook for free.

Ladies, the path to reconnecting with yourself should be a rewarding experience. Don't rush through it. Embrace it. Enjoy spending time with yourself and adding new experiences to your life. Appreciate and fall in love with the woman you discover. Most of all, be proud of yourself for being true to who you are and putting yourself first.

PART THREE

THE NEW DATING JOURNEY

Dating with a Healthy, Confident Approach

CHAPTER 9

PROTECT YOUR PEACE BY ESTABLISHING BOUNDARIES

In a dating expert's social media post asking women's opinions about the current state of online dating, hundreds of women posted comments, and the overall theme among the women was "dating overall is exhausting." The top five issues in their comments were inconsistency, lack of effort, lack of communication, emotional unavailability, and dishonesty. One woman commented that dating was so exhausting, she settled and married her halfway-decent boyfriend to escape single life. Poor girl.

Inconsistency showed up as the central issue in almost half of the comments. Those ladies were fed up with being disappointed by inconsistent men who popped in and out of their lives at their leisure. In the comments, they discussed how they gave men three to five chances to get it right. No, ma'am. You should give no one five chances to prove they can respect you. Why give him a fifth chance when he already showed you four times that he's a "can't get right" man? Now he believes inconsistency is acceptable behavior toward you, so he'll see your chances like bottomless chips and salsa at the cantina. Keep them coming!

You have the power to stop inconsistency by drawing a bold boundary line. Think about why you're allowing the behavior. Did you have a temporary lapse in judgment, or are you afraid of being alone?

Inconsistent behavior is a red flag. The man is subtly informing you of how the duration of the relationship will go. *Believe him!* Men are on their best behavior to win you over in the early stages of dating. If he's inconsistent at his best, honey, six months later, his inconsistency will leave you tormented with anxiety and walking around pulling your hair out.

Ladies, lately some men have developed the attitude that we should be grateful to be chosen by them, like we should stand in line yelling, "Pick me!" They have been poisoned by wounded male influencers who persuade them to treat us disrespectfully and get us to disregard our boundaries in order to break us down. These grown men put women down and try to convince us we are damaged goods for having life experience. Like my mom would say, "That's a lie from the pits of hell." You're allowed to have boundaries.

When I fixed my self-worth and value issues, I developed a higher level of awareness and a lower level of tolerance for foolishness. My patience with inconsistent men was short. I called them out on their behavior. I hadn't before because I was afraid that they would walk away, but now, my peace is more important than having a man in my life. The days of giving men multiple chances to treat me right are over. Chances equal wasted time, and I do not have time to waste.

Ladies, men will test you to see what they can get away with. When I went back onto a dating app, I met this handsome dark-chocolate professional. We talked on the phone and texted each other for a few days until he stopped communicating. I figured he wasn't interested, so I didn't reach out to him either. Seven days later, he sent a text message: "I see you ghosted on me." *Wait. What?*

Do you see this manipulation? We hadn't communicated

with each other, but he tried to make it my fault. I responded, "I can say the same for you, but I don't see it that way. We both quit communicating."

He replied, "Okay yeah . . . lol." *What?* He did not know what to say after his blame-shifting tactic failed.

I responded, "If you're interested in getting to know me, we can resume talking, but it has to be consistent." I never heard from him again. He was not interested in a woman who would hold him accountable.

I had a similar communication issue with a man a few weeks later. He told me he had clashed with the last woman he was with because she didn't allow him to lead in the relationship. We communicated for three weeks until I noticed some odd behavior. Whenever we talked on the phone, he was on the road. We never spoke on the phone at night or when he was home relaxing. Over the three weeks we talked, I would not hear from him for days at a time. I made him aware that we were getting to know each other, and that we must communicate to do that. He apologized and said he would do better.

One night, we attempted a FaceTime call, but he took too long to show up, so I went to sleep. I texted the next day and said, "Let's try again tonight." He didn't respond. Four days later, he sent a text telling me he had typed the message to ask me to FaceTime, but forgot to hit send. That was an insult to my intelligence, so I did not respond. Let's get the issues with his story straight: One, why would he have messaged me to ask me to FaceTime when I had already messaged him? Two, why didn't he just call me on FaceTime if he had thought he had texted me? And three, either way, why didn't he text or call for another four days after that night? I would've been a damn fool to believe him. *Block!*

Since my matches were not going well on my preferred dating app, I switched to an equally popular app that I hadn't tried before. There I met Kyle, a tall, decent-looking dad. I had seen him around on the dating apps I swung back and forth on for about a year. We matched once, but it wasn't good timing for me. When we matched again seven months later though, it was perfect timing.

Kyle and I communicated regularly on FaceTime. Our conversations were clean and casual, nothing too serious. After two weeks, Kyle and I met at an outdoor restaurant for a date. As we sat across from each other, he kept reaching over to grab my hand or leg. He was too touchy. The server came to take our drink orders, and I asked for water.

Kyle asked, "You're not drinking?"

"No. I'm not."

"Why not?"

"Because I don't want to."

Kyle seemed to be annoyed that I didn't want alcohol. *Red flag.* He also joked about my long clip-in extensions not being my hair. I had worn the same hair on our FaceTime, and it blended perfectly, so I didn't understand the problem. *Red flag #2.*

Considering Kyle's judgmental and immature nature, we were not a match. When we exited the restaurant, he asked for a hug. To be nice, I extended my arm for a side hug, but he went in for a full-front hug . . . and with both of his big hands wide open, he grabbed my butt and squeezed. Furious, I yelled, "Excuse you! What made you think you could do that? You haven't earned the right to touch me like that."

I never gave him the impression we were at that level—ever. He asked, "Who do you think you are? If a man has to wait to earn the right to touch your booty, you will be single for the rest of your life."

Lord have mercy. Again, I was done. I said, "Well, I'd rather be single for the rest of my life than have your hands on me again."

When I got home, I had a little bit of a setback and wondered if I overreacted. Healing is a journey, ladies. Of course I hadn't overreacted. That dude was disrespectful and nasty, and he overstepped a common-sense boundary.

On that same dating app, I met Jason. He messaged, "What a beautiful smile. I'd like a chance to get to know you if that's okay with you."

"I'm cool with that," I responded.

We chatted about the basic "get to know you" questions, then he asked if we could FaceTime. I told him it wasn't the best time since I had had a cardio day at the gym earlier and my hair was a mess. For five minutes, he insisted and assured me that if my face looked the same, my hair didn't matter. Ladies, don't fall for that.

My hair was in a raggedy ponytail with a leopard-print headband to cover the front. It wasn't the first live view of me I would want any man to see. Jason started a FaceTime call anyway. He could not take no for an answer. I know I didn't have to answer, but I did and told him that FaceTiming me without permission was not cool. He apologized and said I looked fine, and then immediately he slammed me with a Q&A session. "How many children do you have? What are their ages? How many live at home?" Jason's voice was dry and serious. I don't remember him smiling at all.

He continued and asked when my last proper relationship had been. "I had a three-month sort-of relationship that ended almost two years ago."

In a judgmental tone, he asked, "So you accepted a sort-of relationship?" *Obviously I didn't, smart tail.*

"No; I moved on and learned from it."

"Are you ready for a real man?" he asked.

"Can you clarify what you're really asking me?"

"Are you ready for a real relationship?" he redirected.

"Oh, okay. Why didn't you ask that?"

In the nastiest tone, Jason said, "It's my question, and I can ask it however I want."

Sis, I threw in the towel. "I can see that we're not a good match," I informed him. "We would bump heads a lot." He had the nerve to ask if I was sure. *Hell yeah, I'm sure!*

Listen, when a man oversteps your boundaries in the early stages of dating, depending on the seriousness, set or reset a clear boundary so they can know exactly what you don't allow. However, sometimes you will have to cut them off the first time.

Each one of those men overstepped my boundaries. When I reset expectations with the man who communicated inconsistently and he continued to do it, he crossed the line. His inconsistent behavior was disrespectful and gave me a glimpse into the frustrations of dating him. A man like Kyle, who thinks he is entitled to your body, does not deserve a resetting of expectations or a second chance. Such behavior shows arrogance and a lack of self-awareness and can become dangerous. Last, Jason showed a lack of respect by calling me on FaceTime when I asked him not to.

These examples may seem small to some of you, but subtle behaviors are a preview to show you what a person is capable of.

Before doing the work to heal, I thought of myself as a "go with the flow" type of person, and I used that mentality as an excuse for why I had few to no boundaries in relationships. You can't have a healthy dating life without healthy boundaries, and that was a big part of why my dating life was usually unhealthy. When I reconnected with myself and rediscovered my value, my perspective changed. Instead of going with the flow, I created the flow.

If you struggle with establishing boundaries, I want you to get your journal and do this exercise. On a blank page, create two columns. Label one side *What I Currently Tolerate* and on the other side, write *What I Will No Longer Tolerate.* Write as many items on your list as you like. This will help you to clearly process what you've been accepting as normal behavior that's been harmful to you and change your expectations. Commit to upholding your boundaries, and remember that you created them to protect yourself.

CHAPTER 10

GETTING TO KNOW YOU: IDENTIFYING YOUR WANTS AND NEEDS

The woman in the last chapter who married her "halfway-decent" boyfriend settled because she was convinced she couldn't find someone better . . . or better yet, someone better wouldn't find her. She will have to live with her decision and make the best of a not-so-good situation. Based on my experience in settling, I can confidently say she will have more bad days than good. So, how do you make sure not to make this same mistake? Know exactly what you want and why it's important to you. I could see this more clearly after doing the inner work, since I was no longer looking through the lens of desperation. Often, we go about dating without putting much thought into it. We know we want someone to love and do life with. But connecting our lives to someone else's deserves deeper consideration than just asking ourselves if they can show us a good time. It's much more serious than that.

To be successful in getting the type of man and relationship you want, get deeply attuned to yourself. Ladies, we naturally take on the role of the nurturer and easily become attuned to the needs of those we love, but we often struggle to identify and express our own needs. A clear understanding of your wants, needs, negotiables, and deal-breakers equips you to be clear on your expectations and to date thoughtfully.

For example, let's say it's important for you to marry a man who doesn't have children. This is important because you want to have a family without outside distractions. You meet a man who checks all your boxes and appears to meet your wants and needs, but he has a young child. Let's determine if this is negotiable or a deal-breaker. You date the man and become annoyed (not jealous) each time he communicates with his child's mother because you think of your potential husband being connected to another woman for a lifetime. If this is something you can't fathom dealing with, it is a deal-breaker. By moving forward with this man, you would likely set yourself up for disappointment or a failed relationship.

When I first started online dating, I set filters to not show men under five feet, ten inches tall, and this was not negotiable for me. One day though, I met a man while standing in a long line at the mall. He was handsome, hilarious, and five foot eight. I gave him my phone number without hesitation because he had an outstanding personality. That day, I changed the height filter on my dating app account. Ladies, I know we get sensitive about height, but should it really be a deal-breaker? I'm sure I passed up a lot of good men under five foot ten by filtering them out. At five feet, three inches short, all I need is to stand next to a man who won't be shorter than me if I wear four-inch heels.

Do you know yourself well enough to be certain of your wants, needs, negotiables, and deal-breakers? I'll share some of mine and give more examples of how to determine yours.

FINANCES

No matter how much money you make, the way you manage it determines the amount of financial stress in your life. I know people who earn comfortable salaries but live paycheck to paycheck. In my twenties, I was irresponsible with money. I gambled money away at the casino that I should've used to pay bills and debts that went into collections. I was buried under a pile of debt.

Once I came to the reality that I needed help, I took a free money management course and took the steps to get my finances under control. I paid all my debts and increased my credit score by almost two hundred points. Ultimately, I created a financial portfolio, including stocks, cash savings, and investments that I take pride in. I started late in my adult years, but it's never too late to get your finances under control.

While I was chatting with a man I met on a dating app, he mentioned he had a $300 debt in collections that he refused to pay. He didn't dispute it. He said he wasn't ready to pay it yet, since he was saving for a seventy-five-inch television. I couldn't believe what I had heard. This forty-something-year-old man cared more about a big-screen television than his credit. Well, that was my last conversation with him.

My expectation of any man who comes into my life is that he is financially stable and understands money and credit. That is nonnegotiable. He doesn't have to have a seven-figure bank account, but he does need to have a plan in place for securing his future.

Financial incompatibility is a major cause of stress and disagreements in marriage and often leads to divorce. What are your expectations for a partner concerning finances? Seriously consider this now so you can prevent it from becoming an issue when you're deep into a relationship.

CAREER GOALS AND AMBITION

There was a point in my life when my vision of the type of lifestyle and future I wanted for myself and my family shifted.

I was tired of having just enough. I joined the military and took advantage of the opportunities to learn new skills and go to college for free. Before I got out, I completed my bachelor's degree and acquired transferable skills in human resources to continue my career as a civilian. Accomplishing those goals required hard work that kept me up for long hours many nights.

My ex-husband appreciated my work ethic, but he couldn't wrap his brain around the magnitude of work and hustle it took to reach the level of success I desired to achieve. His inability to relate to my drive and ambition caused him to question if my goals were selfish. He believed I accomplished enough to relax and live comfortably. Contrarily, I didn't respect his low expectations of me or himself and his lack of goals, drive, and ambition. I felt like I was alone in wanting to create a better life for our family. This caused a lot of problems in our marriage.

Be honest with yourself about your expectations for drive and ambition. If you aspire to build an empire with your partner, don't date a man who doesn't exhibit the drive and desire to build with you. No matter how much of a good person he is, you can't hope a man into being someone he's not.

RELATIONSHIP PREFERENCE

Uncertainty about relationship preference is a deal-breaker for me. I'm absolutely sure I want to get married again. It would be a waste of time for me to entertain anyone who is unsure about marriage.

One charming man I met appeared to be my ideal type. After a week of conversation, he told me he had been married twice and was about 95% sure he wouldn't do it again. The leftover 5% was open for a woman who could persuade him to marry again. It was not in my interest to persuade any man to do something he was 95% sure he didn't want to do. In my early thirties, I might've accepted that as a challenge, but in my forties, ain't nobody got time for that. I had to let him go.

On the first phone call, I let men know that I'm dating with the purpose of meeting the man I will marry. This is not intended to apply pressure. I do it to be transparent and weed out the men who aren't looking for the same. I've heard people say to wait a few weeks to tell a man you want marriage or to wait for him to bring it up because mentioning it too early will scare him away. I disagree with that. It's better to be up front and discuss it sooner rather than later. If your honesty scares a man away, it's because his intentions aren't aligned with yours, and that's okay.

FAMILY

Between my mom's seven children, sixteen grandchildren, and in-laws, we all look out for each other. It's not often that we're all together at the same time, but when we are, it's a party. The love you can feel around my family amazes people. My four sisters and I are best friends who speak in our own language made up of a compilation of references to movies and '90s sitcoms. We talk on FaceTime or our text group every day.

Obviously, family is important to me, and when I meet someone new, I ask about how well they get along with theirs. I understand that not everyone's family shares the closeness my family does, but if they don't get along at all, I wonder if they will be capable of accepting how I prioritize mine.

Family dynamics can be tricky, so this is negotiable for me. Some people don't get along with their families for legitimate reasons, but it is worth finding out why to avoid potential problems in the future, especially if you plan to build a family of your own with someone.

FAITH

It's a requirement for me that the man I'm connected with has a relationship with God. He should share my Christian beliefs and take prayer seriously. If religious beliefs and spirituality are serious to you, carefully consider what is and isn't a deal-breaker.

Separate beliefs may mean you attend separate churches. Depending on how serious you both are about your faith, religion can become a constant debate and end up causing division in your household. Consider how important this is to you and the impact it could have on your relationship before you get into a serious one.

As you develop your expectations for a future partner, remember to set expectations for yourself. You should reflect the qualities you are seeking. If you require a man with a fit body—note the word *require*—your body should be fit as well. If you require a man with a successful business or career, he may expect the same level of success from you. Make your expectations reasonable.

To increase your chances of getting your happily ever after, stand firm to your wants and needs. Create a solid set of standards so you can have a clear way of determining whether someone measures up to them. If, after reading this chapter, you find that you're unsure of what your wants and needs are, take a break from dating and devote some time to finding out.

CHAPTER 11

ONLINE DATING RULES AND TIPS

They say experience is the best teacher. Based on my experience with online dating for seven years, I've learned a lesson or two . . . and I have established some best practices along the way that I'll share with you. If you're considering trying online dating, or if you've already tried it and didn't have the best experience, my tips on getting your profile set up and going on your first date may be helpful to you. Start with answering a few questions. Are you ready to date? Think about it and be honest with yourself. Have you done the work to heal so you can date with a confident mindset? Did you recently experience a breakup? Reflect and make sure you're not beginning to date without resolving issues that could impact a new relationship. What are you looking for in a man?

Be sure of your wants and needs and be realistic with your expectations. If you need help with this, go back to chapter ten to read about how to sort out your negotiable and nonnegotiable qualities. If you're still unsure, consider dating with the expectation of discovering what you like and dislike.

What type of relationship do you want? Maybe you want to date for fun with no expectations, or you may be looking for a serious relationship that leads to marriage. Think about it, and be honest with yourself. Make this clear to your prospects from the beginning. If you're unsure of what they're looking for, don't be afraid to ask. Remember, respect your own time.

Depending on specific preferences, religion, ethnicity, the type of relationship you want, and the age group you're in, there's a dating app to fit almost anyone's needs. My favorite dating app was one where men couldn't send a message until the woman reached out first. I preferred this because I didn't get the ridiculous number of unwanted messages I received on other sites. A simple internet search of *best dating apps for [whatever you're looking for]* will yield a list of results to get you started.

Whether it's here in this chapter, or from a wise friend, get guidance on how to navigate the online dating world before setting up a dating app profile. People argue that meeting online does not differ from meeting at the grocery store, but they're wrong. When you meet someone in the grocery store, you know that they're real, what they look like, and how their voice sounds, while when you meet someone online, they may be a completely different person. It's more of a gamble to meet someone online; you're much more likely to meet a scammer or get catfished or ghosted. Understanding what to expect and how to handle these types of situations can save you some time and heartache.

CREATE YOUR PROFILE

The most important thing to remember when creating your profile is to be honest. Deception will catch up with you, so it's best to avoid it from the start. Ladies, get a friend to take your pictures or purchase a ring light with a small Bluetooth remote. A ring light will show you in the best lighting and prevent you from having to add too many filters. Adding filters is fine but filtering to significantly alter your facial features or body parts is dishonest and will set you up for disappointment.

Upload a photo of you doing something you enjoy, one of you doing something interesting, and one of you outdoors. Show that you have a life.

Upload at least one full-body picture to your profile. Don't be shy about showing your curves or skinny thighs. If there isn't a full-body picture on your profile, a man will either swipe past you or match with you and ask for one. Don't be offended. We all have our preferences, and he's trying to see if you fit his. Eventually, the man will see the real you on video or in person. Don't waste your time—or his—hiding the real you.

Your bio should be brief and hit the key points of who you are and what you're looking for. Put your personality on display. Use your wit and humor and save the serious stuff for your matches. Take advantage of the free profile features. You have the option on some dating apps to select from a list of conversation prompts. Use this to give potential matches an idea of the type of person you are. Watch out not to provide too much information. There are dating apps that provide prompts to list more about you but be careful about the information you give. There's a lot that a person can do with a little personal information.

THE SWIPE

Before you swipe right or send a message to anyone, there are some things to look out for. The first thing we see are pictures. If a photo looks like it's out of a magazine, it probably is. It may be a bot or a fake profile. Don't entertain it. Blurry pictures likely were taken years before good cell phone cameras. Before I knew better, I entertained a man with slightly fuzzy photos. He looked young and fit. On our first phone call, his voice didn't match the look of the guy in the photos. He spoke to me like he was my granddaddy. The first thing he told me after *hello* was, "Nah, I know you got a church home. What church you go to?" He sounded like Mr. Brown in a Tyler Perry movie. I asked him to send me a picture while we were on the phone. His picture exactly matched the person I was talking to. He was short, stocky, had lots of gray hair, and had on suspenders—exactly what I had pictured in my mind. He *was* Mr. Brown. Be leery of abnormal-looking pictures. If you choose to give the guy a chance, ask him to send a recent picture or to have a video call.

It's tempting to swipe right upon seeing an attractive face and sexy physique, but do a profile audit to read the entire profile first, if there's anything to read. I didn't match with men who didn't take the time to write anything on their profiles. *It's lazy!* If they write nothing in the bio, I assume they're boring and there isn't anything interesting about them, or they're arrogant and think their looks are enough.

Dissect profiles to find red flags. You can easily spot red flags in a bio. A guy wrote, "Y'all mfs so out of shape. It would be a waste of time and a disappointment to even try." I wish you could see this man. He was shirtless and looked like he had an extra-large bowling ball in his stomach. The nerve of him to say anyone was out of shape! Even if he was fit, his comment was rude and nasty. And he thought I would match with him with verbal abuse red flags flying all around him? *Ha!*

Ladies, I understand men get just as frustrated as we do in dating, but it doesn't help when they approach us with a chip on their shoulder. This man said, "I've been living in this city for eight years, and I give up. Too many tricks have the majority of women here rotten! There's too much lying and perpetrating on this app. You don't want a man; you want a child and someone to put up with your BS." *Bitter much?* We don't need those bad vibes. Ladies, use wisdom. If it howls like a wolf, it's a wolf.

Have you ever told a man who approached you in a public place that you weren't interested, and he followed you around, asking why not? That rarely happens, but it's common on dating apps. Men you're not interested in will approach you. Write back and thank them for their message and tell them you're not interested. If they write back, don't feel obligated to respond. If they won't stop sending messages, block them. Men hate rejection and some can't take no for an answer. Case in point . . .

A man who attempted to match with me praised himself in his bio for being handsome, ripped, and an overall great catch. When he sent a message and I wrote back my generic thank-you message, the guy did not take it well. He sent multiple messages, asking me why I was attracted to him and rambled on about why I should be grateful that he had chosen me. It was creepy, so I blocked him. He found me on another dating app and resumed sending messages, asking why I was attracted to him. I reported him. Poor guy was super hot with major insecurity issues.

Hear me. You will see lots of attractive men, but save the "swipe right" for the ones who pass the profile audit. Remember, analyze his pictures, read his entire profile, and don't ignore the red flags.

AFTER THE MATCH

Once you match, it's time to start chatting. Exchange messages on the dating app for at least three days to determine whether you're interested in the guy. If the chat goes well, take your conversation offline. I don't recommend sharing your personal phone number right away. In chapter two, we discussed the amount of personal information someone can find out about you with your phone number. To be careful until you build trust, use an app such as Google Voice for texting and making phone calls. The app is free, and you'll get a phone number that connects calls to your personal phone number. If you choose to get a Google Voice number, make sure to turn off the default setting labeled *call screening*. I found out about this setting when a guy I had given my number to told me he was about to hang up the phone because he thought he was calling a prison when he was asked to state his name to have the call connected. I guess he called prison often.

If the phone call goes well, schedule a video call. Now, you may encounter men who make excuses for why they can't get on a video call with you—don't go any further. They're most likely hiding something. Be cautious of men who can never video call when they're home. They might not live alone. People are on dating apps for different reasons. Some are married or in relationships and will suck up your time and chat with you every day with no intention of ever speaking or meeting in person. I've seen it happen.

You also don't have to share your personal phone number to make video calls. If you're an iPhone user, you do have to share your personal phone number to use FaceTime, but to avoid sharing your personal number, download Google Duo to make video calls. Snapchat is also a common app used for video chatting. Most dating apps have voice and video call capability through the app, but I haven't used one that works well. Besides, most dating coaches will tell you to get off the app as soon as possible. I agree. If a guy has to open the app to communicate with you, he might get some swipes in while he's there, and you might do the same.

Something to keep in mind when preparing for your first video call with a match is that first impressions are everything. Make sure you look like your profile picture. If you have on makeup in all your profile pictures, put your makeup on for the call. When you look like your pictures, he'll be relieved to know he's not being catfished and will gain a bit of trust in you. Be prepared to step back so he can get a full view of you and ask him to do the same. Confirm that you're talking to the same person and the same *version* of the person you see in the profile pictures.

Pace yourself when you meet someone you like. Keep your conversation to a maximum of one hour for two reasons. First, no matter how good the conversation is, an hour is a lot of time, and your time is valuable. I learned a hard lesson when I conversed with a man for two hours on our first phone call. At the end of the call, he told me he had enjoyed our conversation and was excited about seeing things grow between us. That was the last time I heard from that man. I wasted a two-hour chunk of my life on entertaining him. Never again will I give that much time to one conversation in the early stages of dating.

Another reason to pace yourself is to prevent developing a false sense of closeness that'll cause you to prematurely lower your guard. Have you ever talked to a man for a week but felt like you've known him for months? It's a familiar feeling you get when you have a lot in common or you spend a large amount of time with someone early on. Keep in mind that you don't know the man. Don't mistake comfort for trust. It's common for some men to create a false sense of trust or love bomb you to gain control and get you to loosen your boundaries. Sis, stay vigilant and keep yourself in check.

Chat with multiple people. Putting all your focus on one person or all your eggs in one basket is not ideal for online dating. I know most women aren't comfortable chatting with more than one man, but it's likely that, if you don't, you'll be giving all your attention to a man who is splitting his attention between you and several other women. You might waste time talking to one man at a time.

There are men on dating apps who seem to be great catches but are only there to play. Keep your options open until you've met someone in person and established a solid connection. Then you can focus on that one person.

MEET IN PERSON

Ladies, once you feel a connection with a guy, meet him in person. You should do so when you're comfortable, but as soon as possible after you've spoken consistently for a week. Talking for weeks doesn't compare to meeting face-to-face. Remember my meeting with Hot Boost? I met a totally different person than the one I had spoken with on the phone for weeks. In person, you have the opportunity to interact and to see how he interacts with others. Listen to how he speaks to others and what he says, and observe his attitude.

Schedule a meet and greet to take place when you're ready. A meet and greet is a short meeting to discover if there's any chemistry between you and the man you have an interest in. Keep the meeting at a maximum of two hours. You may want to stay longer, but don't. End it and take some time to process how the meeting went. Refrain from communicating for a couple of hours to give the man time to process it as well. If he felt a good vibe, he will want to see you again. He'll contact you to schedule a date.

Safety is extremely important in online dating. Be cautious and protect yourself at all times. Women have been assaulted by men they've met online. Most of those stories have one of two things in common: they either met for their first date at a home or hotel, or they drove in the same car. There's no good reason to be in either of those situations on a first date.

Your first few dates should be in public places, and someone should always know where you're going and who you're with. When I had a first date, I sent my sisters a screenshot of my date's dating app profile and shared my location on my phone. I would make it known to my date that people knew where I was and who I was with. If you're thinking this is extreme, you're right; it is. You can never be too careful when your life depends on it.

ONGOING COMMUNICATION

Match the energy of the man you're dating. If he's communicating regularly, keep it going. If you notice you're the one reaching out first or he sends one-word responses to your lengthy messages, stop. When his communication with you gets shorter, he may be communicating more with someone else. Give him a chance to show his interest in you. If he gives excuses for why he can't talk and why he can't see you, express your concerns and give him a chance to fix his behavior. But if he continues the behavior, move on.

I've heard women say that online dating is hard. I understand their pain because I used to feel the same way. It wasn't until I created rules and boundaries around my dating life that my experience changed. Have you established any rules that make navigating online dating less frustrating for you? If you don't, that's okay. You're in the right place. You can adopt mine or use this chapter as a guide to create some. Grab your journal. Starting from the section titled "The Swipe," reread or skim through this chapter and write down rules that work for you. You can date without having any rules at all, but having some and following them will make navigating online dating easier and less stressful. Of course, if you need more guidance with creating your rules, I have you covered. Week 6 of my signature coaching program, Love YOU Harder and Date Smarter, focuses on building a rule system that works for you, and this is also always something that I'm glad to explore with my 1:1 clients. Find out more at **Love YOU Harder and Date Smarter:** www.seanmariebee.com/loveyouhardergroupcoaching/

FINAL THOUGHTS

Often, dating apps get stamped with a bad reputation. Unfortunately, they cannot control the fact that most subscribers haven't taken the time to heal from past issues and are not in a healthy space to date. Those unhealed people who use dating apps create a less-ideal experience for themselves and others. Since you've made it to the end of this book, you're now equipped with the tools and knowledge to change your experience for the better. Let's discuss the key points you should take away from this book and implement into your life to improve your self-love and change your online dating experience for the better.

In chapter one, you learned to identify, acknowledge, and address red flags and got familiar with some examples of behaviors to look out for. Ignoring red flag behaviors won't make them go away.

Chapter two covered the steps for running a background check on your dates through simple internet searches and paid and free background-check sites. Don't skip the background check—you never know, you may find something that can save you from heartache.

In chapter three, we discussed ghosting, what to do and what not to do when it happens to you, and how to handle ghosters when they come back.

Chapter four provides insight into how settling for an emotionally unavailable man becomes the perfect setup for getting pulled into a situationship.

Chapter five covered how allowing desperation and anxiety to drive your choices results in forcing a relationship to work with someone who isn't right for you.

In chapter six, we discussed doing the inner work to identify and address negative self-beliefs and their possible causes.

Chapter seven explores the role that sex plays in developing new relationships and how decisions we make concerning sex are triggered by internal and external factors.

Chapter eight focuses on the importance of reconnecting with yourself, appreciating all of who you are, and creating your ideal life.

In chapter nine, we discussed creating boundaries in your dating life, how to effectively communicate them, and how to handle when someone crosses them.

Chapter ten is a guide to help you discover your wants, needs, negotiables, and deal-breakers to attract the right man for you.

Chapter eleven serves as a guide for navigating online dating and establishing rules that work for your pace and are comfortable for you.

I wrote this book because I was compelled to share my experiences with you. By changing my negative self-view, I loved, valued, and appreciated myself in a way that would no longer allow me to settle for mediocre and poor treatment in dating—or from myself. I became more vigilant, confident, and protective of myself, creating a better experience overall. I hope this book includes everything you need to improve your dating experience and break down the barriers standing in between you and the love you deserve. If this is something you desire but don't believe you can do on your own, I'm here for you. Visit my website, seanmariebee.com, to find out how my coaching can support your journey.

END

ABOUT THE AUTHOR

Sean Marie Bee, a certified life coach specializing in self-love and online dating, is the founder of Unclouded Love Coaching for women. Sean Marie helps single women refine their most important relationship—with themselves. Her affinity for helping others is also displayed in her extensive career in Human Resources coaching and developing employees and in her eight years of service in the US Army. She resides in Houston, Texas, with her three young adult children. Sean Marie loves hearing from her readers and enjoys discussing issues women encounter in online dating.

To connect with her,
visit **www.seanmariebee.com**.

AUTHOR'S NOTE

Thank you for reading this book. I nervously pondered how many of my personal thoughts, emotions, and experiences I wanted to share with the world when I first started writing it. I was afraid of being judged. But later, I came to the realization that I wasn't writing this book for me, that I wasn't writing to simply tell stories. I was writing this book for all single women who were frustrated with dating and didn't understand what they were doing wrong.

I knew this book would not fully serve its purpose if I wasn't transparent in what I shared, so I didn't hold back. What I didn't know was that this book would help me gain the confidence to coach other women to overcome their barriers in dating.

I would love to know what you learned from this book and how it has helped you in any way. You can tell me by clicking on the link below and leaving a review. I would truly appreciate it. I can't wait to read it!

Leave a US Amazon review:
Seriously, This Is Online Dating?

Made in United States
Orlando, FL
07 May 2022

17634967R00082